or before

basic
FRENCH
grammar

Other titles in this series:
Basic German Grammar by John Clapham   0 7195 7122 7
Basic Italian Grammar by Tony Giovanazzi   0 7195 8501 5
Basic Spanish Grammar by Richard Leathes   0 7195 7120 0

© Valerie Worth-Stylianou 1996

First published 1996
by John Murray (Publishers) Ltd
50 Albemarle Street
London W1X 4BD

Layouts by D&J Hunter
Typeset by Wearset, Boldon, Tyne and Wear
Typeset in 11/12pt Galliard and 9/12pt Frutiger
Printed and bound in Great Britain by The University Press, Cambridge.

A CIP record for this book is available from the British Library.

ISBN 0 7195 7121 9

basic
FRENCH
grammar

Valerie Worth-Stylianou

JOHN MURRAY

for Anastasia and Christopher

I'd like to thank Carolyn Burch and Talya Baker for
all their encouragement, advice and practical support

CONTENTS

▼▼▼
INTRODUCTION

The aim of this book is to make the main points of French grammar accessible and easy to remember for anyone wishing to learn or revise them. It takes a very straightforward approach and does not assume that you are already familiar with grammatical terms.

- The purpose of each rule and structure is clearly explained.
- Examples taken from everyday language show how each point is applied and help you to remember the way it works.
- Activities give opportunities to practise or revise each point; answers to the activities are provided.

Basic French Grammar is ideal for independent revision or study, or to use alongside other course materials for reference and practice. It will be invaluable if you are in any of the following learning situations:

- working towards a language qualification or examination;
- taking a language component as part of a broader course such as business studies;
- brushing up on your French in preparation for a holiday or business trip to a French-speaking country;
- improving your grasp of French for use at work.

▼▼▼
NOUNS & ARTICLES
names of people, places and things

▼ Articles

An article is a word used in front of a noun to mean *a, the, some, any*. The words which are in bold in the passage below are all articles. You will see that sometimes you need an article in French even though there is not one in English (and occasionally vice versa). This will be explained in the following sections.

Aujourd'hui **les** touristes ont appris que **la** ville de Narjac a décidé de leur offrir **des** billets gratuits pour **les** voyages en bus pendant **le** mois d'août. **Un** Allemand nous a dit: «C'est **une** excellente idée, nous pourrons prendre **le** bus pour circuler en ville, et il n'y aura plus de queues devant **les** parkings!»

Today tourists learned that the town of Narjac has decided to give them free tickets for bus journeys in the month of August. A German gave us his opinion: 'It's an excellent idea, we can take the bus to travel around the town, and there won't be any more queues to get into the car parks!'

▼ *Le, la, l', les = the – the definite article*
In French, the form of the definite article – the word meaning *the* – changes depending whether it is used with a noun which is masculine or feminine, singular or plural.

There are four forms of the word *the* in French:

- **le** for a masculine singular noun beginning with a consonant:

le chien, le jardin, le sac

- **la** for a feminine singular noun beginning with a consonant:

la carte, la pomme, la table

- **l'** for a masculine or feminine singular noun beginning with a vowel or **h**:

l'été, l'homme, l'olive

A very few words beginning with **h** are an exception, and need **le** or **la**. The most common are:

la haie = *hedge*, le hall = *hall*, le haricot = *bean*, la Hollande = *Holland*

- **les** for any plural noun:

les enfants, les mères, les pères

If you learn the definite article with a new noun it will help you to remember the gender.

▼ Activity 1 *Put in the definite article*

Choose the correct form of le/la/l'/les to complete each gap.

A partir du 24 juin, ... *Journal du Temps* vous offre . . . . météo des plages. Il va vous donner . . . . température de l'air, par exemple, et vous dire si . . . . eau est trop froide pour se baigner. . . . . gens veulent savoir si . . . . soleil est plus fort . . . . matin ou . . . . après-midi, aussi. . . . . semaine dernière, on a annoncé . . . . retour du beau temps sur toute . . . . France après . . . . pluie du mois de mai.

▼ *Saying to the/at the:* à + *the definite article*
There are four forms for saying to the/at the:

- **au** for a masculine singular noun beginning with a consonant:

au chien = *to/at the dog*
J'ai lancé la balle **au chien**.   *I threw the ball to the dog.*

- **à la** for a feminine singular noun beginning with a consonant:

à la gare = *to/at the station*
Je vais vous attendre **à la gare**.   *I'm going to wait for you at the station.*

- **à l'** for a masculine or feminine singular noun beginning with a vowel or an **h**:

à l'hôtel = *to/at the hotel*
Tu vas rentrer **à l'hôtel**?   *Are you going back to the hotel?*

- **aux** for any plural noun:

aux filles = *to the girls*, aux garçons = *to the boys*
Elle parlait **aux filles ou aux garçons**? *Was she speaking to the girls or the boys?*

▼ Activity 2   à + *definite article*

Translate the words in brackets into French:

a   Elle parlait (to the) policier.
b   J'ai couru (to the) téléphone.
c   Vous avez écrit (to the) autorités?
d   Tu viens (to the) cinéma?
e   Je vous retrouverai (at the) magasin.
f   Il a laissé son sac (at the) piscine.
g   Pourquoi sont-ils (at the) hôpital?
h   Elle a envoyé un fax (to the) clients.

▼ *Un/une = a/an – the indefinite article*

There are two forms of the word for *a/an* in French:

- **un** for a masculine noun:

un oncle, un jour

- **une** for a feminine noun:

une idée, une voiture

■ Un/une = a/an and the number 'one'

J'ai un chat et une souris.   *I have a cat/one cat and a mouse/one mouse.*

▼ *Du/de la/de l'/des = some/any – the partitive article*

There are four forms of the word meaning *some/any* in French:

du for a masculine singular noun beginning with a consonant:

du lait, du sucre

- **de la** for a feminine singular noun beginning with a consonant:

de la salade, de la pluie

- **de l'** for a masculine or feminine singular noun beginning with a vowel or an **h**:

de l'eau, de l'huile

- **des** for any plural noun:

des gâteaux, des maisons

▼ *Du/de la/de l'/des = of the*
These same forms are also used to translate *of the* (= **de** + definite article):

Quel est le nom **du Président**?   *What's the name of the President?*
Je veux acheter une carte postale   *I want to buy a postcard of the*
de l'église.   *church.*

but when a sentence is negative, the forms **du, de la, de l', des** must be replaced by **de** (just as *some* is replaced by *any* after a negative in English):

Elle veut du lait, mais elle **ne veut**   *She wants some milk, but she*
pas de pain.   *doesn't want any bread.*

de also replaces **du, de la, de l', des** after the expression **ne . . . plus** (*no more*):

Vous voulez des boissons fraîches?   *Do you want some cold drinks?*
Je **n'ai plus d'**Orangina, mais j'ai du   *I haven't got any more Orangina,*
Coca.   *but I've got some Coke.*

▼ Activity 3   *Du, de la, de l', des*

Use the correct form of *du, de la, de l', des, de* to fill each gap.

Un enfant difficile
–   Maman, j'ai faim!
–   Qu'est-ce que tu veux, chéri?
–   . . . . gâteaux et puis . . . . chocolat!
–   Mais je n'ai pas . . . . chocolat. Tiens, voici . . . . abricots.
–   Non, je ne veux plus . . . . abricots, j'en ai trop mangé hier.
–   Bon, alors tu veux quelque chose à boire peut-être?
–   Oui, je veux . . . . bière!
–   Pascal, arrête, sois sérieux!
–   Alors je veux . . . . limonade.
–   Mais je n'ai plus . . . . limonade. Tiens, j'ai . . . . eau.
–   Dis donc, maman, si on allait dans ce café, on pourrait choisir . . . . glaces.
–   Tu as déjà mangé trois glaces aujourd'hui, et puis moi, je n'ai plus . . . . argent!

▼ *When to include the article*

There are some important differences between English and French when it comes to including or leaving out the article.

- You do *not* use **un/une** in French when you are giving someone's profession or status:

Mon frère est étudiant et ma soeur est médecin.	*My brother's a student and my sister's a doctor.*
Il y a une réduction si vous êtes retraité.	*There's a reduction if you're a senior citizen.*

- Normally you do *not* need **un/une/des** after **sans** (= *without*:

Comment est-ce qu'on y arrive sans voiture?	*How do you get there without a car?*

but if **sans** is followed by a noun with an adjective, you do need **un/une/des**:

Elle l'a fait sans un seul ami.	*She did it without a single friend.*

- You *do* need to include **le/la/les** in front of abstract nouns (i.e. words like: 'joy', 'sadness', 'patience'):

La patience et **la** générosité sont toujours importantes.	*Patience and generosity are always important.*

- You *do* need to include **le/la/les** in front of nouns which refer to a general group of people or general type of thing:

Les petites voitures polluent moins que **les** gros camions.	*Small cars cause less pollution than big lorries.*

- You *do* need to include **le/la/les** before the names of countries:

La France a plus de châteaux que l'Australie.	*France has more castles than Australia.*

but if you use **de** (= *from*) or **en** (= *in*) before the name of a country, you *do not* need **le/la/les**:

Il est revenu **d'**Italie?	*Has he come back from Italy?*

- When you use an adjective to describe a word like 'day', 'week', 'month', 'year' you *do* need **le/la/les**:

Vous serez où **l'**année prochaine?	*Where will you be next year?*
La semaine dernière il était malade.	*Last week he was ill.*

- In French you normally need **le/la/les** to refer to parts of the body, where in English we use '*my (arm)*', '*her (eye)*', etc.

Fermez les yeux!   *Shut your eyes.*

- You *do* need to include **des** (meaning *some*) in front of plural nouns, even though we often leave out 'some' in English:

Pour mon anniversaire j'ai reçu **des** vêtements et **des** CDs.   *For my birthday I got clothes and CDs.*

■ Repeating the article

When you have two or three nouns together, in French you must repeat the article in front of each noun:

Nous avons vu **des** bateaux et **des** hélicoptères.   *We saw some boats and helicopters.*

Remember that if the nouns are in the singular, you need the correct form of the article for each noun:

Je dois acheter **du** café, **de la** limonade et **de l'**eau minérale.   *I must buy coffee, lemonade and mineral water.*

▼ Activity 4   *When to include the article*

Decide whether you need an article in each of the blanks. If so, put in the right word. If not, put an X:

- Excusez-moi, Madame, je peux vous poser quelques questions?
- Oui, bien sûr, vous êtes . . . . reporter?
- Non, je suis . . . . détective. Alors, vous travaillez ici, Madame?
- Oui, je suis . . . . secrétaire.
- Vous étiez ici . . . . semaine dernière?
- Oui, sauf vendredi.
- Et jeudi vous avez vu . . . . enfants qui jouaient près du magasin?
- J'ai vu . . . . garçons avec . . . . chien.
- Ils étaient habillés comment?
- Je ne sais pas. Si, il y en avait un sans . . . . imperméable qui s'était maquillé . . . . visage.
- Et que faisaient-ils?
- Ils regardaient . . . . voitures dans . . . . parking.
- Ah bon. Je vous remercie, Madame.

▼ Masculine and feminine nouns

All nouns in French are either masculine or feminine. It is obvious that **un homme** (*a man*) will be masculine and **une femme** (*a woman*) will be feminine, but you simply have to learn the gender of nouns that refer to things, places, feelings, etc.

It helps to learn new words with the article **un** or **une**, so that you remember the gender.

▼ Activity 5   *Spot the gender*

Look at the nouns which are underlined in this passage. Make a list of those that are masculine and another list of those that are feminine.

Un <u>dimanche</u> ils m'ont invité à une <u>fête</u> de famille. Ils habitent une grande <u>villa</u>, pas loin de la <u>plage</u>. Nous avons mangé dans le <u>jardin</u>, sous un énorme <u>pommier</u>. Pour commencer il y avait un <u>assortiment</u> de crudités, puis comme plat principal on avait du <u>poulet</u> rôti avec de la <u>salade</u>. Bien sûr le <u>père</u> de Céline avait sorti une bonne <u>bouteille</u> de Bordeaux de la <u>cave</u>! Et au <u>dessert</u> il nous a proposé du <u>champagne</u> pour accompagner la <u>glace</u>.

There are rules that help you to remember the gender of some groups of nouns:

- Words referring to men are masculine and words referring to women are feminine:

un acteur = *an actor*   une actrice = *an actress*
un ami = *a (male) friend*   une amie = *a (female) friend*

Common exceptions:
Four nouns are always feminine even when they refer to men:

une connaissance = *an acquaintance*   une personne = *a person*
une vedette = *a (film) star*   une victime = *a victim*

Regarde, cet homme est une vedette! Tu le reconnais?   *Look, that man's a star. Do you recognise him?*

- Languages are masculine:

le français = *French*   le portugais = *Portuguese*

• Days of the week, months and seasons are masculine:

le lundi = *Monday*   un été ensoleillé = *a sunny summer*

• Countries are usually feminine if they end in -**e**, masculine if they do not:

la France, la Belgique   le Portugal, le Canada

• Fruits and vegetables are feminine if they end in -**e**, masculine if they do not:

une pomme, une courgette   un melon, un haricot

Common exceptions:
un concombre = *a cucumber*   un pamplemousse = *a grapefruit*

▼ Activity 6   *Work out the gender*

Put *le* or *la* in each of the gaps:

a   Charles n'est pas . . . . personne que je voulais voir.
b   . . . . Chine et . . . . Japon ont signé le document.
c   Tu veux apprendre . . . . latin?
d   Nous devons contacter . . . . tante ou . . . . grand-père de Michel.
e   J'ai un cours de danse . . . . mardi soir.
f   . . . . Suisse et . . . . Luxembourg reçoivent beaucoup de touristes.
g   . . . . printemps est une belle saison en Normandie.
h   Tu veux prendre . . . . poire, ... banane ou . . . . kiwi?
i   Cet homme n'est pas . . . . victime.
j   Attendez, on va couper . . . . tomate et . . . . concombre en morceaux.

▼ *Masculine endings*

Usually nouns are masculine if they have one of the following endings:

-**age** le courage, le garage
-**at** le chocolat, le candidat
-**ing** le shopping, le parking (mostly 'franglais')
-**isme** le fascisme, le tourisme
-**ment** le commencement, le parlement

Common exceptions
la cage, une image, la nage, la page, la plage, la rage

▼ Feminine endings

Usually nouns are feminine if they have one of the following endings:

-ade la limonade, la promenade
-aison la maison, la raison
-ance la confiance, la tolérance
-sion/-tion la confusion, la situation
-té la capacité, la société
-tude une attitude, la solitude

Common exceptions

le comité = *committee,* le côté = *side,* un été, le pâté, le traité = *treaty*

▼ Activity 7   *Work out the gender*

Put *le* or *la* in each of the gaps:

a   . . . . shampooing n'est pas dans la salle de bains.
b   C'est . . . . saison des festivals.
c   Je ne peux pas manger . . . . chocolat.
d   Quelle est . . . . solution que vous préférez?
e   . . . . promenade a été très agréable.
f   Il faut traverser . . . . village pour arriver à . . . . plage.
g   . . . . solitude te fait peur?
h   Tu dois signer . . . . document.
i   Je ne regarde jamais . . . . télévision.
j   . . . . sincérité est . . . . qualité la plus importante.

■ Words with two genders

There are a few cases where the same word is found in both the masculine and the feminine gender, but with different meanings. Here are the most common:

un livre = *a book*	une livre = *pound (money/weight)*
un mode = *way, method*	une mode = *fashion, style*
un page = *a pageboy*	une page = *a page (in a book)*
un poste = *a job/TV or radio set*	la poste = *post office*
un tour = *a turn, trick, tour*	une tour = *a tower*
un voile = *a veil*	une voile = *sail (faire de la voile = to go sailing)*

▼ Making a noun plural

To make the plural of most nouns in French, as in English, you add an **s** to the end of the noun:

un livre = *a book*	des livres = *some books*
une valise = *a case*	des valises = *some cases*

but:
- If the singular of the noun already ends in -**s**, -**x** or -**z**, you make no change for the plural:

un héros	des héros
un prix	des prix
un nez	des nez

- Family surnames do not add an **s** in French:

les Cardin = *the Cardins*

- When the singular ends in -**al** the plural form is -**aux**:

un journal	des journaux
un cheval	des chevaux

Common exceptions:

un bal	des bals
un festival	des festivals

- When the singular ends in -**eu/eau** the plural form is **eux/eaux**:

un neveu	des neveaux
un bateau	des bateaux

Common exception:

un pneu	des pneus = *tyres*

- Some nouns with the singular ending in -**ail/-ou** have their plural in -**aux/-oux**. The most common are:

le travail	les travaux = *works/roadworks*
le vitrail	les vitraux = *stained glass windows*
le bijou	les bijoux = *jewels*
le chou	les choux = *cabbages*
le genou	les genoux = *knees*

Most other nouns with the singular ending **ail/-ou** have their plural in **ails/ous**:

un rail	des rails
un trou	des trous = *holes*

- Some nouns have an irregular plural. The most common are:

madame	mesdames
mademoiselle	mesdemoiselles
monsieur	messieurs
un oeil	des yeux

▼ Activity 8   *Plurals*

Put the nouns in brackets in the plural.

a   Tu as vu mes (clé)?

b   Qui a volé les (bijou)?

c   Il y a deux (trou) dans le jardin.

d   Il s'intéresse aux (dinosaure).

e   Je n'en croyais pas mes (oeil).

f   Roger et Charles sont les (héros) du film.

g   Vous avez quels (jeu)?

h   J'aime tous les (animal).

i   Bonjour (Monsieur).

j   Il y a des (travail) sur l'autoroute.

k   Je suis invité chez les (Arnould).

l   Au revoir, (Madame).

▼▼▼
ADJECTIVES
describing people, places and things

Adjectives are words which describe nouns: e.g. a *green* bus, a *large* dog, a *kind* person, an *unusual* present.

Remember that in French adjectives often go after the noun they describe.

▼ Activity 1   *Spot the adjective*

Underline the words which are adjectives in the following passage.

Film à ne pas manquer!

«Voyage en Orient» est un film sensationnel. Il s'agit d'un lieutenant anglais et d'un botaniste français qui se lancent dans une aventure incroyable. Ils espèrent faire le voyage le plus rapide de Londres à Bombay en utilisant l'ancienne route des épices. Mais un homme jaloux essaie d'arrêter cette courageuse entreprise.

▼ Making adjectives agree with the noun they describe

▼ *Regular adjectives*

In French adjectives agree with the noun they describe:

- If the noun is masculine singular, you need the masculine singular form of the adjective:

un vélo **bleu** = *a blue bike*   un film **intéressant** = *an interesting film*

- If the noun is feminine singular, you need the feminine singular form of the adjective:

une voiture **bleue** = *a blue car*   une histoire **intéressante** = *an interesting story*

- If the noun is masculine plural, you need the masculine plural form of the adjective:

des vélos **bleus** = *blue bikes*   des films **intéressants** = *interesting films*

- If the noun is feminine plural, you need the feminine plural form of the adjective:

des voitures **bleues** = *blue cars*   des histoires **intéressantes** = *interesting stories*

You can see from these examples that to make a regular adjective agree, you take the masculine singular form (**bleu, intéressant**) and add the correct ending:

masc. sing.	fem. sing.	masc. pl.	fem. pl.
	-e	-s	-es
bleu	bleue	bleus	bleues
intéressant	intéressantes	intéressants	intéressantes

but:
- If the masculine singular form of the adjective already ends in -**e**, the feminine singular form is the same.

un camion jaune   *a yellow lorry*
une voiture jaune   *a yellow car*

Both the masculine and feminine plural forms add -**s**:

des chapeaux **rouges** = *red hats*   des robes **rouges** = *red dresses*

- If the masculine singular form of the adjective already ends in -**s**, there is no change for the masculine plural form:

des cafés **français**   *French cafés*

and the feminine plural form adds -**es**:

des écoles **françaises**   *French schools*

▼ Activity 2 *Making regular adjectives agree*

Make each adjective in brackets (the masculine singular form) agree
with the noun it describes:

Un jeu télévisé
- Regardez bien cette photo, Madame Xavier. Alors, maintenant
  fermez les yeux, et vous allez nous la décrire.
- Il y a deux enfants devant une (grand) ferme. Le garçon porte un
  pullover (jaune) et une veste (noir), je pense . . .
- Non, la veste est (gris).
- Ah bon! La fille qui est plus (petit) porte une robe (vert) et des
  chaussures (vert) aussi.
- Très bien. Vous avez dix points! Continuez!
- Euh, la ferme est (joli), il y a beaucoup de fleurs (rouge) devant la
  porte. Je crois que la porte est (ouvert).
- Non, elle est (fermé), mais ça n'a pas d'importance. Vous avez 16
  points déjà. Avec 20 points vous pouvez gagner un prix
  (formidable)!
- Ah, oui, à côté de la ferme on voit de (gros) canards très (drôle) qui
  vont plonger dans l'eau.
- Ça y est! Vingt points! Vous êtes (brillant), Madame Xavier! Vous
  venez de gagner une semaine (gratuit) au soleil! Bravo!

▼ *Variations on regular forms*

For five common groups of adjectives, the feminine or plural
forms follow slightly different rules:

masc. sing.	fem. sing.	masc. pl.	fem. pl.
-f	**-ve**	**-fs**	**-ves**
un caractère vif	une réaction vive	des caractères vifs	des réactions vives
-x	**-se**	**-x**	**-ses**
un mari jaloux	une femme jalouse	des maris jaloux	des femmes jalouses
-al	**-ale**	**-aux**	**-ales**
un monument national	une route nationale	des monuments nationaux	des routes nationales

-el	-elle	-els	-elles
un problème personnel	une raison personnelle	des problèmes personnels	des raisons personnelles
-en	-enne	-ens	-ennes
un nom ancien	une maison ancienne	des noms anciens	des maisons anciennes

Common exceptions
un coup **fatal**, une bataille **fatale**, des coups **fatals**, des batailles **fatales**

▼ **Activity 3** *Making adjectives agree (variations on regular forms)*

Make each adjective in brackets (the masculine singular form) agree with the noun it describes:

a Le film dépend des effets (spécial).
b Il faut aller en Grèce si tu aimes l'histoire (ancien).
c Vous menez une vie (actif)?
d Pour les petites routes, il faut consulter une carte (départemental).
e Vous faites des danses (traditionnel)?
f Combien de centres (international) y a-t-il?
g Raoul raconte des histoires (fabuleux).
h 'Mon Pays' vend des produits (régional).
i Jacqueline a entendu une nouvelle (sensationnel)!
j Les vedettes de cinéma sont souvent (mystérieux).

▼ *Irregular adjectives*
You need to learn the forms of the following common irregular adjectives:

Masc. sing.	Fem. sing.	Masc. plural	Fem. plural	Meaning
beau	belle	beaux	belles	*beautiful*
nouveau	nouvelle	nouveaux	nouvelles	*new*
vieux	vieille	vieux	vieilles	*old*
fou	folle	fous	folles	*mad*
bon	bonne	bons	bonnes	*good*
épais	épaisse	épais	épaisses	*thick*
gentil	gentille	gentils	gentille	*kind*
gros	grosse	gros	grosses	*big, fat*

long	longue	longs	longues	*long*
grec	grecque	grecs	grecques	*Greek*
public	publique	publics	publiques	*public*
turc	turque	turcs	turques	*Turkish*
blanc	blanche	blancs	blanches	*white*
frais	fraîche	frais	fraîches	*fresh, cool*
sec	sèche	secs	sèches	*dry*
doux	douce	doux	douces	*sweet, gentle*
neuf	neuve	neufs	neuves	*new*

■ Masculine singular forms of *beau, nouveau* and *vieux*

The adjectives **beau** (*beautiful*), **nouveau** (*new*) and **vieux** (*old*) have a second form for the masculine singular, used when the adjective comes immediately before a noun beginning with a vowel or before a noun beginning with **h**. Here are both forms of these adjectives:

Regular Masc. sing.	Before a vowel/h Masc. sing.
beau	bel
nouveau	nouvel
vieux	vieil

Vous avez de la chance. Vous habitez un **beau** quartier, et vous avez un **bel** appartement.	*You're lucky. You live in a beautiful area, and you have a beautiful flat.*
Elle a acheté un **nouveau** poste de télévision et un **nouvel** ordinateur.	*She's bought a new television set and a new computer.*
J'ai vu un **vieux** chien et un **vieil** homme.	*I saw an old dog and an old man.*

Question: What do you do about making adjectives agree when the same adjective describes more than one noun?

Answer: If the nouns are both masculine, use the masculine plural form of the adjective:

Le film et le livre sont très **amusants**.	*The film and the book are very amusing.*

If the nouns are both feminine, use the feminine plural form of the adjective:

Ma mère et mes tantes sont **fatiguées**.	*My mother and my aunts are tired.*

If the same adjective describes both masculine and feminine nouns, use the masculine plural form of the adjective:

Elle a trois enfants. Le premier garçon et la fille sont déjà **indépendants.**

She has three children. The first boy and the girl are already independent.

▼ **Activity 4** *Making regular and irregular adjectives agree*

Make each adjective in brackets (the masculine singular form) agree with the noun it describes. Some of the adjectives are regular, others are irregular – check the list above.

Un artiste veut partir en vacances

Dans l'agence de voyage

– Bonjour, Monsieur, je peux vous aider?
– Oui, je veux passer mes vacances à l'étranger.
– Alors, vous pensez à quel pays?
– Ah, vous savez, je suis artiste, alors il me faut un (beau) appartement, des températures (doux), de (long) journées (ensoleillé), et la lumière (blanc) du matin . . .
– La Grèce peut-être?
– J'y ai passé de (bon) vacances, je suis resté chez une famille (grec), très (gentil). J'ai même acheté une moto toute (neuf). Mais je veux connaître d'(autre) pays.
– Et la Turquie? Tenez, j'ai cette (nouveau) brochure, et les prix sont très (bas).
– Oui, mais je veux un (vieux) hôtel, loin des plages (public). Je crois que les hôtels (turcs) sont (plein) de touristes . . . J'ai horreur des touristes, ils sont (fou)! Vous savez ce qui arrive? Je choisis un (beau) endroit (tranquille), des maisons (blanc), le contraste avec la terre (sec), je suis sur le point de commencer mon tableau, et puis des touristes arrivent avec des enfants (impossible)!

▼ *When an adjective does not agree with the noun*
Here is a list of the most important cases when adjectives do *not* agree with the noun(s) they describe:

• colour adjectives (e.g. **rouge**, **bleu**) used with words like *light* (**clair**), *dark* (**foncé**) or *bright* (**vif**):

Vous préférez cette veste-ci qui est **bleu vif**, ou celle-là qui est **vert clair**?	*Do you prefer this jacket which is bright blue, or that one which is light green?*
Vous avez des chaussures **gris foncé**?	*Do you have any dark grey shoes?*

The form for *navy blue* (**bleu marine**) does not agree either:

Il portait une cravate **bleu marine**.	*He wore a navy blue tie.*

* a few simple colour adjectives never agree (i.e. they are invariable and have only one form):

cerise = *cerise, cherry-coloured*	crème = *cream*
lilas = *lilac*	marron = *brown*
orange = *orange*	saumon = *salmon-pink*

J'ai perdu une valise **marron** et deux sacs **orange**.	*I've lost a brown case and two orange bags.*

■ Which word for *brown*?

There are two words for *brown*. You use **marron** when you are describing objects, and it is always invariable:

des chaises marron	*brown chairs*

but you use **brun** to describe hair, eyes and skin. **Brun** is a regular adjective and agrees with the noun it describes

Elle a les yeux bruns.	*She has brown eyes.*

If you want to say someone is sun-tanned, use the adjective **bronzé** which is regular and agrees with the noun it describes:

Angélique est bronzée après ses vacances.	*Angelica is brown/tanned after her holiday.*

---

* in some expressions involving **grand-** + feminine noun, **grand-** does not agree:

grand-chose = *much, something* (used after a negative)

Je n'ai pas trouvé grand-chose.	*I haven't found much.*

la grand-mère = *grandmother*

Ma grand-mère est vieille.	*My grandmother is old.*

(but note **les grands-parents**)

■ **Phrases where adjectives do not change**

In a number of common idioms, adjectives are used with a verb (i.e. like an adverb). In these cases, the adjective never changes. Here is a list of the most important of these idioms:

parler **bas** = *to speak quietly*
sentir **bon** = *to smell good*
travailler **dur** = *to work hard*
parler **fort** = *to speak in
  a loud voice*

coûter **cher** = *to be expensive*
payer **cher** = *to pay a lot*
aller/continuer **tout droit** = *to
  go/carry straight on*
sentir **mauvais** = *to smell bad*

▼ Activity 5 *Do these adjectives need to agree?*

Translate the following phrases into French. Some of the adjectives agree, but others do not – check the list above. The nouns you need are in the box below.

a   a blue suitcase and brown shoes
b   a navy blue tie
c   a black jacket and light green gloves
d   red shoes and dark grey socks
e   The cakes smell good.
f   She is working too hard.
g   Go straight on!
h   The apples are expensive.

la chaussette	la chaussure	la cravate	le gant
la pomme	la valise	la veste	le gâteau

▼ Position of adjectives

▼ *Adjectives after the noun*

In French the adjective normally goes after the noun:

un cheval noir, un trou profond, une idée affreuse
a black horse, a deep hole, a terrible idea

Sometimes you may find that writers will put a particular adjective in front of a noun for stylistic effect, but this is not usual style. You should put adjectives after the noun they describe, unless they belong to one of the groups listed in the next section.

Note: When there are two (or more) adjectives following the same noun, they must be joined by **et**:

C'était une journée froide et pluvieuse. | It was a cold, rainy day.

▼ *Adjectives before the noun*
Five important groups of adjectives go before the noun they describe:

- *my,* (**mon, ma, mes**), *your* (**ton, ta, tes**), etc. – *possessive adjectives* (see pages 24–26).

C'est mon vélo. | It's my bike.
Où sont tes lunettes? | Where are your glasses?
Je ne vois pas leur voiture. | I can't see their car.

- *this, that, these, those* (**ce, cet, cette, ces**) – *demonstrative adjectives* (see pages 26–27).

Regarde cette maison! | Look at this/that house!
Ces amis arriveront plus tard. | These/Those friends will arrive later.

- Adjectives describing numerical order (**le premier, le deuxième, le dernier**):

Tu as vu les premiers résultats des élections? | Did you see the first results from the elections?
On cherche un quatrième homme. | They're looking for a fourth man.

- Indefinite adjectives: i.e. words like

autre (autres) = *other*
chaque = *each*
quelque (quelques) = *some, a few*
  (used mainly in plural)

un certain (une certaine) = *a certain*
plusieurs = *several, a few*
tel (telle, tels, telles) = *such*
tout (toute, tous, toutes) = *every, all*

Il voulait poser une autre question. | He wanted to ask another question.
J'ai pris quelques photos. | I've taken a few photos.
Voici toute la famille. | Here's all the family.

- The following common, short adjectives:

beau = *beautiful*
bon = *good*
bref = *brief, short*
grand = *big*
gros = *fat, big*
haut = *high*
jeune = *young*
joli = *pretty*

mauvais = *bad*
meilleur = *better*
moindre = *least*
nouveau = *new*
petit = *small, little*
sot (sotte, sots, sottes) = *foolish, silly*
vaste = *vast*
vieux (vieille, vieux, vieilles) = *old*

▼ **Activity 6**   *Putting the adjective in the right place*

Choose suitable adjectives from the selection given in the box and add at least one adjective to each of the nouns given in bold type. There may be several correct answers.

a   Maman, où est le <u>train?</u>
b   . . . <u>jardin</u> appartenait à mon grand-père.
c   Elle regardait un <u>programme</u>.
d   Nous avons trouvé les <u>sandales</u> dans le <u>magasin</u> après le <u>port</u>.
e   Les <u>chiens</u> étaient dans le jardin.
f   Les <u>maisons</u> sont vendues.

petit	rouge	mon	vieilles	ce		nouveau
abandonné	vieux	vaste	grecques	troisième		toutes

▼ *Adjectives used before and after the noun with different meanings*

Some adjectives can be used before and after the noun, but their meaning changes according to their position. Here is a list of the most common ones:

Adjective	Meaning before noun	Meaning after noun
ancien	*former/old* une ancienne église *a former church*	*ancient/old* un monument ancien *an ancient monument*
cher	*dear* (= loved) mon cher neveu *my dear nephew*	*dear/expensive* un magasin cher *a dear/expensive shop*
dernier	*last* (of a series) le dernier jour des vacances *the last day of the holidays*	*last* (= most recent) la semaine dernière *last week*
grand	*great* un grand ami *a great friend*	*big, tall* un homme grand *a tall man*
même	*same* la même personne *the same person*	*-self* le directeur même *the director himself*

pauvre	*poor* (sympathy)	*poor* (no money)
	le pauvre chat!	une famille pauvre
	the poor cat!	*a poor family*
propre	*own*	*clean*
	ma propre chaîne hi-fi	une cuisine propre
	my own stereo	*a clean kitchen*
seul	*single/only*	*alone*
	une seule pièce de 10F	un enfant seul
	a single ten-franc coin	*a child alone**
sale	*nasty*	*dirty*
	une sale histoire	une chambre sale
	a nasty affair	*a dirty room*

* *an only child* = un enfant unique

▼ Making comparisons with adjectives

- To say *more* interesting, kind*er*, etc. (the comparative form of the adjective), use **plus** in front of the regular form of the adjective (which still agrees with the noun):

des voisins gentils = *pleasant neighbours*
des voisins **plus** gentils = *pleasanter neighbours*

- To say *less* interesting, *less* kind, etc., use **moins** in front of the regular form of the adjective (which still agrees with the noun):

des voisins **moins** gentils = *less pleasant neighbours*

Question: How do you say *more. . . . than* or *less . . . . than?*
Answer: You use the comparative form of the adjective **+ que:**

Ma grand-mère est plus âgée   *My grandmother is older*
que mon grand-père.   *than my grandfather.*

- To say the *most* interesting, kind*est*, etc. (the superlative form of the adjective), use **le plus/la plus/les plus** in front of the regular form of the adjective (which still agrees with the noun):

les voisins **les plus** gentils   *the most pleasant neighbours*

- To say the *least* interesting, *least* kind, etc., use **le moins/la moins/les moins** in front of the regular form of the adjective (which still agrees with the noun):

les voisins **les moins** gentils   *the least pleasant neighbours*

> ■ **The most. . ./the least. . . in (the world)**
> To say *the most/the least. . . in the world/in my class*, etc. you
> need to use **de** (= of) to translate *in*:
>
> C'est le plus beau jardin du monde.   *It's the most beautiful garden in*
>   *the world.*
> Annick est l'élève la moins   *Annick's the least organised child*
> organisée de la classe.   *in the class.*

The adjective **bon** has irregular comparative and superlative forms:
meilleur, meilleure, meilleurs, meilleures
le meilleur, la meilleure, les meilleurs, les meilleures.

C'est un bon disque.   *It's a good record.*
C'est un meilleur hôtel.   *It's a better hotel.*
C'est la meilleure course du monde   *It's the best race in the world.*

The adjective **mauvais** has regular comparative and superlative
forms:

Cette photo est encore plus   *This photo is even worse.*
mauvaise.
Voici les plus mauvais résultats de   *These are the worst results of the*
l'année.   *year.*

You may also come across irregular comparative and superlative
forms of **mauvais: pire, le pire, la pire, les pires:**

C'est le pire jour de ma vie.   *It's the worst day of my life.*

• To say *as . . . as*, use **aussi . . . que**. The adjective agrees with
the noun(s) it describes in the normal way:

Ces salles sont aussi grandes que les   *These rooms are as big as the*
autres.   *others.*

To say *not as . . . as* use **pas si . . . que**. The adjective agrees
with the noun it describes in the usual way:

Ces salles ne sont pas si grandes   *These rooms are not as big as the*
que les autres.   *others.*

▼ **Activity 7**   *Making comparisons*

Translate the words in brackets in the conversation:

Conversation avec un petit cousin

- Dis, Charlotte, tu es (bigger than me)?
- Oui, bien sûr.
- Tu es (as big as my mother)?
- Pas tout à fait. Pourquoi?
- Parce que moi je suis (the smallest in the family) et c'est embêtant. Pour le football, mes frères sont toujours (better than me). Papa et maman sont (stronger than me), il n'y a que le chien qui est (not as strong)!
- Et qu'est-ce que tu veux faire, mon pauvre Daniel?
- Je veux être (the best footballer in the world) et (the best artist in my class), et je veux être (as tall as you)!

▼ Mon, ma, mes, ton, ta, etc. (= my, your, etc.) – possessive adjectives

In French possessive adjectives always go before the noun they describe:

ma soeur = *my sister*   notre chalet = *our chalet*

Because the words for *my, your*, etc. are adjectives, they have different forms to agree with the noun they describe.

Note: The adjective always agrees (masculine/feminine, singular/plural) with the noun it describes, *not* with the owner of the noun.

If the noun is masculine singular, the word for *my* is **mon**:

mon stylo = *my pen*   mon argent = *my money*

If the noun is feminine singular beginning with a consonant, the word for *my* is **ma**:

ma tasse = *my cup*   ma montre = *my watch*

But if the noun is feminine singular beginning with a vowel/**h**, use **mon**:

mon orange = *my orange*   mon humeur = *my mood*

If the noun is plural (masculine or feminine), the word for *my* is **mes**:

mes chaussures = *my shoes*   mes pieds = *my feet*

Here is a table showing all the possessive adjectives:

| | Describing a noun which is | | |
	Masc. sing.	Fem. sing.	Masc. pl./Fem. pl.
MY	mon	ma*	mes
YOUR	ton	ta*	tes
HIS			
HER	son	sa*	ses
ITS			
OUR	notre	notre	nos
YOUR	votre	votre	vos
THEIR	leur	leur	leurs

* But if the noun is feminine singular beginning with a vowel/**h**, use **mon, ton, son**:

ton encre, son hôtel.

Question: If **son, sa, ses** can mean both *his* and *hers*, how can you tell the difference?

Answer: It's true that, for example, **son album** can mean both *his album* and *her album*. Usually the meaning is clear from the context:

Sophie a pris des photos incroyables. Elle m'a montré son album.   *Sophie has taken some incredible photos. She showed me her album.*

Philippe est inquiet parce que son père est malade.   *Philip is worried because his father is ill.*

But if there is any doubt you can always add **à lui** for *his* and **à elle** for *hers* after the noun:

Est-ce que c'est **sa** chemise **à elle**?   *Is it her shirt?*

Ce ne sont pas **ses** baskets **à lui**, n'est-ce pas?   *They're not his trainers, are they?*

■ Talking about parts of your body

When you are talking about parts of your body, you will not use *my, your*, etc. as often in French as you do in English. Usually, you need **le, la, les** (the definite article), before a part of the body:

Je dois me laver **les** mains. *I must wash my hands.*
Mon frère s'est cassé **le** bras. *My brother broke his leg.*

With the common idiom **avoir mal à** (= *to be hurting*), you will need the forms **au, à la, à l', aux**:

J'ai mal **au** genou. = *My knee hurts.*
Elle a mal **à la** gorge. = *She's got a sore throat./Her throat is hurting.*
Vous avez mal aux pieds? = *Are your feet hurting/sore?*

▼ Activity 8   *Possessive adjectives*

Translate into French the words in brackets:

a Où as-tu mis (his) clés?
b Elle a perdu (her) photo.
c Ils ont vendu (their) vélos.
d Charles, je peux emprunter (your) gomme?
e Quand est-ce que vous vous lavez (your) cheveux?
f Elle a oublié (her) manteau.
g Ma mère a rangé (our) chambre.
h Il a réparé (his) machine.
i (My eyes are hurting)
j (Is your leg sore?)

▼ Ce, cet, cette, ces (= this, that, these, those) – demonstrative adjectives

The words *this, that, these, those* are demonstrative adjectives. They must agree with the noun they describe.

• If the noun is masculine singular beginning with a consonant, use **ce**:

ce soir = *this/that evening*   ce billet = *this/that ticket*

- If the noun is masculine singular beginning with a vowel or **h**, use **cet**:

cet article = *this/that article*   cet hiver = *this/that winter*

- If the noun is feminine singular, use **cette**:

cette fenêtre = *this/that window*   cette réunion = *this/that meeting*

- If the noun is plural, use **ces** (for masculine and feminine):

ces tables = *these/those tables*   ces bancs = *these/those benches*

Question: If **ce/cet/cette** mean both *this* and *that*, how can you tell the difference?

Answer: In lots of cases you don't need to distinguish between *this* and *that*, which is why there is only one word in French. However, if you have a sentence where the contrast is important, you still use **ce/cet/cette/ces**, but add **-ci** (= *this, these*) or **-là** (= *that, those*), to the end of the noun:

Je ne voulais pas **ces gâteaux-là**. Regardez, **ces gâteaux-ci** sont meilleurs.	*I didn't want those cakes. Look, these cakes are better.*
Qu'est-ce que vous préférez, Madame, **cette couleur-ci** ou **cette couleur-là**?	*What do you prefer, Madam, this colour or that colour?*

▼ Activity 9   *Demonstrative adjectives*

Put the correct form of *ce/cet/cette/ces* in each of the gaps:

Pour aller au centre-ville, c'est simple. . .

- Pardon, Monsieur, pour aller au centre-ville, s'il vous plaît?
- Vous voyez . . . . arbre-là, à côté de . . . . feux? Prenez . . . . petite route, oui, la première avant . . . . grandes maisons. Elle vous mènera au centre-ville. Ah, non, j'ai oublié, il y a des travaux! Alors, vous pouvez faire comme . . . . voiture – vous voyez? – . . . . homme qui double . . . . camion. Vous allez jusqu'à . . . . rond-point, puis vous prenez la route à gauche après . . . . hôtel, tout de suite avant . . . . magasins, oui, ... boulangerie et . . . . café. Enfin, ce n'est pas compliqué et c'est bien indiqué!

ADVERBS
describing where, when and how something is done

Adverbs are words which usually describe a verb. In English a large number of adverbs, though not all, end in -*ly*:

He stopped **suddenly**.   She sang that very **well**.

Adverbs can also describe an adjective or another adverb:

She was **particularly** interested   I can't visit you **very** often.
in this match.

In French adverbs are invariable. This means that they only have one form, so (unlike adjectives) they do *not* agree with anything.

▼ Forming adverbs from adjectives

▼ *Regular forms*
A large number of adverbs describing the manner or way in which you do something (softly, easily, mysteriously, etc.) are formed from the corresponding adjective (soft, easy, mysterious, etc.). You need to take the *feminine singular* form of the adjective and add the ending -**ment** for the adverb:

Adjective (fem. sing.)	Adverb	Meaning
douce	doucement	*softly*
facile	facilement	*easily*
mystérieuse	mystérieusement	*mysteriously*

Question: What happens if the adjective has an irregular form in the feminine singular?

Answer: Unless the adjective and adverb belong to one of the groups of irregular forms (pages 29–30), the feminine form of the adjective, regular or irregular, will usually give you the basis for the adverb:

Adjective (fem. sing,)	Adverb	Meaning
cruelle	cruellement	*cruelly*
folle	follement	*madly, foolishly*
sèche	sèchement	*drily*

▼ Activity 1 — *Forming adverbs from adjectives: regular forms*

Complete the following advert by translating the adverbs. The masculine singular forms of the corresponding adjectives are given in the box below. For each one, you will need to form the feminine singular adjective in order to make the adverb.

Essayez notre voiture Galaxie 2000!
Est-ce que vous voulez voyager (rapidly) dans une voiture qui roule presque (silently)? Téléphonez-nous (immediately) pour essayer notre modèle Galaxie 2000! Cette voiture est (miraculously) adaptée aux conditions de la vie moderne. (Naturally), elle est conçue pour vous garer (easily) en ville. Mais nous pouvons (exceptionally) vous laisser prendre l'autoroute avec nous. Là vous allez découvrir (finally) tous les plaisirs d'une voiture performance. (Fortunately) vous pourrez ensuite choisir la Galaxie 2000 vous-même!

rapide	silencieux	immédiat	miraculeux	naturel
facile	exceptionnel	final	heureux	

▼ *Irregular forms*

The following groups follow slightly different rules for forming adverbs:

- A small number of common adverbs formed from the *feminine* singular form of the adjective need an acute accent on the **e** before -**ment** (= -**ément**):

Adjective (fem. sing.)	Adverb	Meaning
confuse	confusément	*confusedly*
énorme	énormément	*enormously*
intense	intensément	*intensely*
précise	précisément	*precisely*
profonde	profondément	*deeply*

- When the masculine singular form of the adjective ends in -**é**, -**i**, -**u**, the adverb is formed by adding -**ment** to this (i.e. using the *masculine*, not the feminine form of the adjective):

Adjective (masc. sing.)	Adverb	Meaning
aisé	aisément	*easily*
vrai	vraiment	*really, truly*

- If the masculine singular form of the adjective ends in **-ant** or **-ent**, the adverb ends in **-amment** or **-emment**:

Adjective (masc. sing.)	Adverb	Meaning
constant	constamment	*constantly*
indépendant	indépendamment	*independently*
fréquent	fréquemment	*frequently*
récent	récemment	*recently*
évident	évidemment	*obviously*

Common exception

lent	lentement	*slowly*

- You need to learn the following very common irregular adverbs:

Adjective	Adverb
bon = *good*	bien = *well*
fort = *strong, loud*	fort = *strongly, loudly, very*
gentil = *kind*	gentiment = *kindly*
mauvais = *bad*	mal = *badly*

▼ Activity 2   *Forming adverbs from adjectives: irregular forms*

Translate the adverbs in brackets into French:

a Mimi voyage (enormously).
b Ma tante lui a dit bonjour très (kindly).
c Il est (really) parti?
d Il travaille (constantly).
e Ces voisins sont arrivés (recently).
f Elle s'est arrêtée (slowly).
g Nous étions (deeply) choqués par son attitude.
h David nage (well).
i Charles s'habille (badly).

▼ Common adverbs of time, place and quantity

A lot of common adverbs, especially those of time, place and quantity, are not based on an adjective. You simply have to learn the French form. You will probably recognise all the adverbs in the examples below:

Souvent les chiens courent **partout**. *The dogs often run everywhere.*
Quelquefois nous avons **beaucoup** de visiteurs. *Sometimes we have lots of visitors.*
Vous avez **trop** travaillé **hier**. *You worked too much yesterday.*

▼ *Beaucoup de, trop de, etc. – adverbs of quantity* + de

There are a number of common adverbs of quantity which are followed by **de** + noun. You will see from the examples that **de** is usually followed immediately by the noun, with *no* article.

assez de = enough
Vous avez assez de place? *Have you got enough room?*

beaucoup de = a lot, much, lots, many
Nous n'avons pas beaucoup de glace. *We haven't got much ice-cream.*

combien de? = how much, how many?
Combien d'argent as-tu? *How much money have you got?*

moins de = less, fewer
Pour ce gâteau, il faut moins de chocolat. *For that cake you need less chocolate.*

peu de = few
Peu de gens le connaissent. *Few people know him.*

un peu de = a little
J'aimerais un peu de fromage. *I'd like a little cheese.*

plus de = more, any more
Il mange plus de fromage que moi. *He eats more cheese than me.*
Je n'ai plus d'enveloppes. *I haven't got any more envelopes.*

tant de = so much, so many
Je n'ai jamais vu tant de touristes. *I've never seen so many tourists.*

trop de = too much, too many
Le boulanger nous a donné trop de croissants. *The baker gave us too many croissants.*

You only need to use the forms **du, de l', de la, des** after these expressions when you want to translate *enough/a little etc. of the . . .*

Vous voulez **plus de** pommes de terre?	*Do you want more potatoes?*

but:

Vous voulez **plus des** pommes de terre que j'ai achetées hier?	*Do you want more of the potatoes I bought yesterday?*

▼ Activity 3   *Beaucoup de, trop de, etc.*

Complete these sentences by translating the words in brackets into French:

a Nous voulons (less) bruit au centre-ville.
b Il faut ajouter (a little) sucre.
c (Few of the) profs ont répondu.
d Il y a (a lot of) vélos.
e Vous voulez (some more) pain?
f (How many) gens arrivent?
g Tu as (so many) livres!
h Elle a mangé (too many) pommes vertes.
i Vous avez (enough) eau?
j Nous voyons encore (many of) nos anciens amis.

▼ Where the adverb goes in the sentence

In French as in English, where you put the adverb often depends on what you want to stress. Both these sentences are correct:

Doucement, elle est entrée sans nous regarder. (stress is on **doucement**)	*Quietly, she came in without looking at us.*

or

Elle est entrée **doucement** sans nous regarder. (less stress on **doucement**)	*She came in quietly without looking at us.*

But there is one important difference between where the adverb goes in English and in French. In English we can put an adverb between the subject and the verb. This is *not* possible in French: the adverb must go **after the verb**:

Si je siffle, mon chien **vient**
immédiatement.
Elle le trouverait **rapidement.**

*If I whistle, my dog immediately
comes.*
She'd quickly find him.

If the verb is in the perfect tense, or the pluperfect, future perfect
or conditional perfect, short adverbs can generally be put between
the part of **avoir/être** (the auxiliary) and the past participle:

Tu as **bien** mangé?
Il était **souvent** allé à Toulouse.

Did you eat well?
He had often gone to Toulouse.

But longer adverbs (say three or more syllables) will be put after
the past participle:

Elle a parlé **couramment.**

She spoke fluently.

▼ Comparisons with adverbs

▼ *To say* more + *adverb, use* plus

Il a répété le mot **plus lentement.**

He repeated the word more slowly.

More . . . *than* = Plus . . . *que*

André joue au tennis plus
régulièrement **que** Mathieu.

*Andrew plays tennis more regularly
than Matthew.*

Three very common adverbs have irregular comparative forms:

Adverb	Comparative form
beaucoup = *much*	plus = *more*
bien = *well*	mieux = *better*
peu = *little/a little*	moins = *less*

Nathalie rit beaucoup.
Nathalie rit plus que sa soeur.

Nathalie laughs a lot.
*Nathalie laughs more than her
sister.*

J'ai bien dormi.
J'ai mieux dormi.

I slept well.
I slept better.

Thierry a peu compris.
Thierry a moins compris.

Thierry understood little.
Thierry understood less.

Question: Doesn't **meilleur** mean *better* too?
Answer: Yes, **meilleur** and **mieux** both mean *better*, but **meilleur** is an *adjective* and **mieux** is an *adverb*. In English *better* is both an adjective and an adverb, which means you have to think how to translate it into French.

If *better* describes a noun (i.e. is an adjective), use **meilleur**, making it agree with the noun it describes:

C'est une **meilleure** chambre.	*It's a better room.*
J'ai trouvé quelques **meilleurs** timbres.	*I've found some better stamps.*

If *better* describes a verb or an adjective (i.e. is an adverb) use **mieux**, which does *not* change:

Vous vous sentez **mieux** maintenant?	*Do you feel better now?*
Cette dame est **mieux** renseignée.	*This lady is better informed.*

▼ *To say* less + *adverb, use* moins

Elle a répondu **moins sévèrement**.	*She answered less severely.*

Less . . . *than* = Moins. . . *que*

Je conduis **moins** souvent **que** ma soeur.	*I drive less often than my sister.*

■ The more . . . the more/the less . . . the less
To say *the more . . . the more* use *plus . . . plus* (remember that you do *not* translate *the* into French):

Plus je lis ce livre, **plus** j'ai envie d'aller au Mexique.	*The more I read this book, the more I want to go to Mexico.*
Plus ils me parlent, **plus** ils m'embêtent.	*The more they speak to me, the more they annoy me.*

To say *the less . . . the less* use *moins . . . moins* (remember that you do *not* translate *the* into French):

Moins je les vois, **moins** je les comprends.	*The less I see them, the less I understand them.*

▼ *To say 'as (+ adverb) as' use* aussi . . . que

Il écrit **aussi bien que** sa cousine.　　He writes as well as his cousin.

▼ *To say 'not as (+ adverb) as' use either* pas aussi . . . que *or* pas si . . . que

Il s'est défendu, mais **pas aussi/pas si courageusement que** Pierre.　　He defended himself, but not as bravely as Pierre.

▼ *To say 'most/the most (+ adverb)' use* le plus
In this structure, **le** never changes.

Véonique a répondu **le plus exactement**.　　Veronica answered most accurately.

▼ *To say 'least/the least (+ adverb)' use* le moins
In this structure, **le** never changes.

Ils parlent **le moins couramment** de tous.　　They speak the least fluently of all.

▼ Activity 4　　*Comparisons with adverbs*

Translate the words in brackets:

Discussion entre deux voisins
- Vous ne pouvez pas jouer de la guitare (more softly)? J'essaie de travailler.
- Mais vous faites du bruit (more often than me)! Et puis je joue (better than you)!
- C'est vrai, mais vous chantez (less well than my cat)! Et je vous dis que je dois travailler.
- Ecoutez, (the more you disturb [*déranger*] me, the more I'm going to sing). Do-ré-mi . . .
- Arrêtez! (The more you sing the more I want to shout [*crier*]!)
- Allez Henri, il faut réagir (more patiently). Et il faut me demander (more politely, less agressively)!
- Écoutez-moi, Paul, je crois que vous devez cacher votre guitare (as quickly as possible), sinon vous allez le regretter!

PRONOUNS
replacing nouns

A pronoun is a word that replaces a noun. Pronouns can refer to people, places or things.

Ma soeur connaît Pascale.
|_____
NOUN

My sister knows Pascale.

Elle la connaît.
 ⟍|
PRONOUN

She knows her.

Le Languedoc produit ces vins.
|_____
NOUN

Languedoc produces these wines.

Il les produit.
 ⟍|
PRONOUN

It produces them.

▼ Personal pronouns

Pronouns can replace nouns in many different ways. All the pronouns in the sentences below are personal pronouns; they replace a noun which names a person or thing.

Tu aimes cette cassette? Louise ne l'aime pas.
Paul et Suzanne n'ont pas d'argent.
Je vais **leur** prêter 100 francs.

Non, le paquet n'est pas pour **toi**!

*Do **you** like this cassette? Louise doesn't like **it**.*
*Paul and Suzanne haven't got any money. I'm going to lend **them** 100 francs.*

*No, the parcel's not for **you**!*

You can see from these examples that personal pronouns can have various forms. Choosing the right form is important to make your meaning clear. Which is the right form? That depends on the job the pronoun is doing in the sentence. The following sections explain this.

▼ Activity 1   *Spot the pronoun*

Which words are personal pronouns in this passage? Underline them.

- Bonjour Lucie. Ça va? Tu es en forme pour ce soir?
- Pas trop, mais j'ai toujours peur avant un concert. Et toi? Marc t'a demandé de l'aider à préparer la salle?
- Ah non, lui, il préfère travailler seul. Je crois qu'il ne me fait pas confiance!
- C'est pas vrai! Tu sais qu'on compte sur toi. Et puis n'oublie pas qu'on va manger au restaurant chinois après le concert!

▼ *I, you, he, etc. – subject pronouns*

A subject pronoun is the subject of the phrase or sentence. In other words, it refers to the person, place or thing which is *doing* or *being* something.

Ils sont sur la table.	*They are on the table.*
Nous sommes arrivés!	*We've arrived!*

Here is a list of all the French subject pronouns:

je	**I**
tu	**you**
il/elle	**he, she, it**
on	**one, we** (see box)
nous	**we**
vous	**you (polite or plural form)**
ils/elles	**they**

Question: How do I know whether to call someone **tu** or **vous**?
Answer: You must always use **vous** when *you* is plural (i.e. you're talking to two or more people):

Chantal et Thierry, **vous** êtes prêts?	*Chantal and Thierry, are **you** ready?*

If you are talking to just one person, use **tu** if the person is a relative, or a close friend, or if you're both young people (say under 20).

But if you're talking to an older person who's not a relative or close friend, you must use **vous** to be polite. So teachers, penfriends' parents, shop-assistants will all be **vous**.

Question: Do I use **il** or **elle** for *it*?
Answer: Use **il** when *it* refers to a *masculine* noun, and **elle** when *it* refers to a *feminine* noun.

Voici le stylo, mais **il** ne marche pas. | Here's the pen, but *it* doesn't work.

Le stylo is masculine.

Tu as vu la mer? **Elle** est très calme aujourd'hui. | Have you seen the sea? *It's* very calm today.

La mer is feminine.

Question: Do I use **ils** or **elles** for *they*?
Answer: Use **ils** when one or more of the people or things *they* refers to is masculine.

J'ai perdu mon carnet de chèques et ma carte de crédit. **Ils** étaient dans mon sac. | I've lost my cheque book and credit card. They were in my bag.

Use **elles** when **all** of the people or things *they* refers to are feminine.

Chantal et Anne ne peuvent pas venir. **Elles** travaillent. | Chantal and Anne can't come. They're working.

■ The subject pronoun *on*
The French use **on** much more than we use *one* in English. Sometimes it means *someone* (you don't know who) or *people* in general, but it is also often used meaning *we*. But remember: **on** always uses the same form of the verb as **il/elle**.

On m'a dit de venir à ce bureau. | *Someone* told me to come to this office.

En Grèce **on** fait une sieste pendant l'après-midi. | In Greece, *people/they/you* have a siesta in the afternoon.

Qu'est'-ce qu'**on** va faire? **On** continue? | What shall *we* do? Shall *we* carry on?

▼ Activity 2   *Subject pronouns*

Change the noun(s) underlined into subject pronouns in these sentences. Look out for cases where you might need to use *on*.

a   <u>Carine</u> est déjà partie?
b   <u>Le café et la pizzeria</u> sont fermés cette semaine.
c   Qu'est-ce que <u>tout le monde</u> va faire ce soir?
d   Pourquoi est-ce que <u>tes cousines</u> ne sont pas venues?
e   <u>Les glaces</u> sont trop chères!
f   <u>Luc et Sylvie</u> travaillent ce soir?
g   <u>Les voitures</u> sont interdites au centre-ville.
h   <u>Une femme dans la rue</u> m'a montré la pharmacie.

▼ *Me, you, him, her, etc. – direct object pronouns*

A direct object pronoun is used instead of a noun as the direct object of the verb. In English the direct object pronoun usually comes immediately after the verb; in French it usually goes immediately before the verb.

Il	aime	la musique.	*He likes (the) music.*
SUBJECT	VERB	DIRECT OBJECT (noun)	

Il	l'	aime.	*He likes **it**.*
SUBJECT	DIRECT OBJECT PRONOUN	VERB	

Tu	ne	**me**	reconnais pas?	*Don't you recognise me?*
SUBJECT		DIRECT OBJECT PRONOUN	VERB	

Here is a list of all the direct object pronouns:

me, m'* = *me*	nous = *us*
le, l'* = *him/it*	vous = *you*
la, l'* = *her/it*	les = *them*
se, s'* = *himself, herself, itself, themselves*	

*Remember that you use **m'**, **t'**, **l'**, **s'** when the next word starts with a vowel (a, e, i, o, u):

Tu **m'**aimes? Oui, je **t'**aime.   *Do you love **me**? Yes, I love **you**.*

Se or **s'** is the direct object of a reflexive verb (see page 82):

Il **se** lave.   *He washes **himself**.*

Question: How do I know whether to use **le** or **la** for *it?*
Answer: Use **le** when *it* refers to a masculine noun, and **la** when
it refers to a feminine noun.

Prends mon sac. Je ne veux   *Take my bag. I don't want to*
pas **le** perdre.   *lose it.*

Le sac is masculine.

Donne-moi ta veste. Je **la**   *Give me your jacket. I'll put it*
mettrai ici.   *here.*

La veste is feminine.

(For the rules about making the past participle agree with the
preceding direct object pronoun, see pages 101–103.)

▼ **Activity 3**   *Pronouns used as direct objects*

Change the nouns underlined into direct object pronouns in these
sentences. Remember that they will go immediately BEFORE the verb.

a   Est-ce que tu achètes <u>les pommes</u> ce matin?
b   Vous n'avez pas vu <u>mon stylo</u>, non?
c   Elle invite <u>ses neveux</u> chaque weekend.
d   Je veux louer <u>la villa</u>.
e   Nous réserverons <u>les places</u>.
f   Tu veux me passer <u>la salade</u>?

▼ *To me, to you, to him/her, etc. – indirect object pronouns*
An indirect object pronoun is used instead of a noun as the
indirect object of the verb. You can tell a noun is the indirect
object because it has the preposition **à** in front of it. In French,
the indirect object pronoun usually goes immediately before
the verb.

Il donnera la valise **à son père**.	*He'll give the case to his father.*

|
INDIRECT OBJECT

Il **lui** donnera la valise.	*He'll give **him** the case./He'll give the case **to him**.*

\
INDIRECT
OBJECT
PRONOUN

Elle parlait **à ses enfants**.	*She was speaking to her children.*

|
INDIRECT OBJECT

Elle **leur** parlait.	*She was speaking **to them**.*

\
INDIRECT
OBJECT
PRONOUN

■ Verbs that are followed by *à* + noun

Some French verbs are followed by **à** (the indirect object) where in English we don't need *to* or *at*:

demander à quelqu'un = *to ask someone*
promettre à quelqu'un = *to promise someone*
téléphoner à quelqu'un = *to telephone someone*

In these cases you will always need to replace **à + noun** by an indirect object pronoun.

J'ai téléphoné **à ma copine**.	*I phoned my friend.*
Je **lui** ai téléphoné.	*I phoned her.*

Here is a list of all the indirect object pronouns for people. (For *to it* and *to them* referring to things and places, see pages 42–43.)

me, m'* = *to me*	nous = *to us*
te, t'* = *to you*	vous = *to you*
lui = *to him, to her*	leur = *to them*
se, s'* = *to himself, to herself, to themselves*	

* Remember that you use **m, t, s** when the next word starts with a vowel (a, e, i, o, u).

Il **m'**a écrit.	*He has written to me.*

Se or **s'** is the indirect object of a reflexive verb (see page 82):

Elle **s'**est dit qu'il fallait partir.	*She said to herself she had to go.*

▼ Activity 4 *Pronouns used as indirect objects*

Translate the words in brackets into French and put them in the correct position to complete these sentences.

a Vous avez parlé déjà? (to her)
b Nous envoyons les livres. (to them)
c Qui a donné cette nouvelle? (to him)
d Vous n'avez pas répondu. (me)
e Je ne parle pas. (to you)
f Je donnerai le cadeau. (them)

▼ Activity 5 *Direct and indirect object pronouns*

Fill in the blanks in this conversation with *le/la/les/lui/leur*.

Voter vert!

– Monsieur Rigaud, vous dites que vous allez voter pour les Verts. Pourquoi est-ce que vous . . . . avez choisis?
– Je . . . . ai choisis d'abord parce qu'ils respectent l'environnement. Moi aussi, je . . . . respecte beaucoup. Les Verts luttent contre la pollution. Dans notre ville, ils . . . . ont déjà réduite. Le centre-ville – vous . . . . connaissez, non? – est devenu une zone piétonne. Moi, j'ai vu le candidat Vert, je . . . . ai écrit même pour . . . . dire que j'étais tout à fait d'accord. Il y a quinze jours, plusieurs membres du parti Vert ont distribué des dépliants sur la pollution industrielle. Je . . . . ai aidés, et je . . . . ai demandé de me recontacter après les élections.

▼ The pronoun *y*

The pronoun **y** is an indirect object pronoun used to refer to a thing or a place (*never* to a person). It usually goes immediately before the verb and is used in two main ways:

• Meaning *there* when you are speaking of a place you are *at* or going *to*.

Ils vont passer un mois à Montpellier. Ils **y** sont arrivés hier.

*They're going to spend a month in Montpellier. They arrived **there** yesterday.*

| Nous allons à la piscine. Moi, j'**y** vais aussi. | We're going to the swimming pool. I'm going there too. |

- To replace **à** + *noun* as indirect object of a verb, when the noun refers to a thing or place.

Vous avez répondu **à sa lettre**?	Have you answered his letter?
Oui, j'**y** ai répondu.	Yes, I've answered it.
Elle a envoyé le paquet **à Lyon**?	Did she send the package to Lyons?
Non, elle ne l'**y** a pas envoyé.	No, she didn't send it there.

■ **More verbs which take à + noun**

Some French verbs are followed by à when English does not need *to* or *at*:

e.g. assister à = *to attend* (an event)
jouer à un sport = *to play a sport*

To replace the noun in these cases you will always need to replace **à +** *noun* by an *indirect object pronoun*:

| Mon frère joue au tennis, et moi j'**y** joue aussi. | My brother plays tennis, and I play *it* too. |

▼ The pronoun *en*

The pronoun **en** usually goes immediately before the verb. It is used to refer to a place or a thing (for the one time it can refer to people see below). It has two main uses:

- **en** replaces **de** + *noun* (referring to place or thing). In this case, **en** is usually translated by *of it/of them*.

| Qu'est ce que vous pensez **des élections**? | What do you think of the elections? |
| Vous me demandez ce que j'**en** pense? Eh bien . . . | You want to know what I think of them? Well . . . |

If the verb is followed by **de** in French, but we do not say *of it/of them* in English, translate **en** simply by *it* or *them*.

Se souvenir de quelque chose = *to remember something*

Tu te souviens de notre premier appartement?	*Do you remember our first flat?*
Oui, je m'**en** souviens très bien.	*Yes, I remember* **it** *well.*

One particular use of **en** to replace **de** + *noun* is to say *away from* a place, or *from* a place:

Les olives qui viennent **de cette région** sont délicieuses.	*The olives which come from that region are delicious.*
Les olives qui **en** viennent sont délicieuses.	*The olives which come* **from there** *are delicious.*

- **En** replaces **du**, **de la**, **des** + *noun*, meaning *some*. In this case **en** can refer to people, places or things:

Vous avez **des tickets de métro**?	*Have you got any metro tickets?*
Oui, j'**en** ai.	*Yes, I've got* **some.**

If a sentence like this is in the negative, **en** will still replace **de** + *noun*, but now it will mean *any*:

Vous n'avez pas **de tickets de métro**?	*You haven't got any metro tickets?*
Non, je n'**en** ai pas.	*No, I haven't got* **any.**

When you are asking or saying *how many* or *how much* of something you have, the pronoun **en** saves you repeating the noun. It means *of it*, *of them*, but often you don't need to translate it in English.

Il n'y a pas assez **de pain**. Tu **en** as mangé beaucoup à midi?	*There's not enough bread. Did you eat a lot (of it) at lunchtime?*

Question: If the English says *I have five*, or *We'll eat two*, and there's no *of it* or *of them*, do I still need **en** in French?
Answer: Yes, you do. When the verb is followed by a number, French always uses **en** if you don't want to repeat the noun.

Vous voulez des oranges? Oui, j'**en** prendrai cinq.	*Do you want some oranges? Yes, I'll take five.*

▼ Activity 6   *The pronouns* y *and* en

Use *y* or *en* to replace the word(s) underlined. Take care to put them in the right place:

a   Il me faut cinq <u>oranges</u>.
b   Vous voulez combien <u>de croissants</u>, Madame?
c   Tu es allé <u>à Cannes</u>?
d   Je n'ai pas besoin <u>d'argent</u>.
e   Vous restez combien de temps <u>dans ce gîte</u>?
f   Je suis partie <u>de l'hôtel</u> vers minuit.
g   Mon frère joue <u>au football</u> ce soir.
h   Ils s'intéressent <u>à ton projet</u>.
i   Elle est responsable <u>de ces équipes</u>.
j   Tu te souviens <u>de nos vacances</u>?

▼ *Where to place direct and indirect object pronouns,* y *and* en

On pages 39–42 we explained that direct and indirect object pronouns and **y** and **en** usually go immediately before the verb.

Elle	en	achète.	*She buys some.*
	|	|	
	PRONOUN	VERB	

Il	leur	parle.	*He speaks to them.*
	|	|	
	PRONOUN	VERB	

If the sentence is in the negative, **ne** goes before the pronoun(s) and **pas** after the verb:

Elle n'en achète pas.	*She doesn't buy any.*
Il ne leur parle pas.	*He doesn't speak to them.*

When you are using a tense formed with **avoir/être** + *past participle* (e.g. the perfect, pluperfect, future perfect, conditional perfect), pronouns must go *before* the part of **avoir** or **être**:

Je **les ai** vus.	*I saw them.*
Nous n'**y sommes** pas allés.	*We didn't go there.*

- If you have more than one pronoun, you need to put the pronouns in the right order before the verb. This table gives you the rules:

1	2	3	4	5	
me	le	lui	y	en	+ VERB
te	la	leur			
nous	les				
vous					
se					

Elle **nous les** a envoyés.	*She sent them to us.*
Vous **y en** avez trouvé?	*Did you find any there?*

- The one time that object and indirect object pronouns and **y** and **en** go *after* the verb is in a positive command (when you are telling someone to do something). In this case, the pronouns are joined to the verb by a hyphen. If you have more than one pronoun after a command, the order is:

COMMAND: *direct object* _ *indirect object* – y–en
                pronoun   *pronoun*

Donne-les-moi!	*Give them to me.*
Servez-vous-en!	*Help yourself to some!*

Did you notice that when **me** would be the last word after the command, it becomes **moi**? Similarly, **te** becomes **toi** and **se** becomes **soi**, but all the other pronouns keep their regular form.

▼ Activity 7   *Where to put object pronouns and* y *and* en

Put the pronouns that are in brackets in the sentence. Take care to put them in the right place and in the right order.

a Elle a vus. (les, y)
b Nous ne parlerons pas. (en, leur)
c Pourquoi est-ce que vous envoyez? (les, nous)
d Tu peux montrer? (la, me)
e Martine a acheté? (en, vous)
f Mes parents ne trouveront pas. (nous, y)
g Offrez! (en, leur)
h Explique! (le, nous)
i Allez! (y)
j Cachez! (les, moi)

▼ Pronouns used for emphasis

Some of the emphatic pronouns (also called disjunctive pronouns) have a different form from the personal pronouns which we have just looked at. Here is a list of the pronouns used for emphasis:

moi = *I, me*	nous = *we, us*
toi = *you*	vous = *you*
lui = *he, him, it*	eux = *they, them*
elle = *she, her, it*	elles = *they, them*
soi = *himself, herself, itself, oneself, themselves*	

Question: How do I know when to use **eux** and when to use **elles** for *they* and *them*?

Answer: If *one or more* of the nouns you are referring to is masculine, use **eux**. But if you are talking about *all* feminine nouns use **elles**.

Pierre et Catherine? Je suis parti sans **eux**.	*Pierre and Catherine? I left without them.*
Françoise et Sophie? Je suis parti sans **elles**.	*Françoise and Sophie? I left without them.*

You need to use pronouns for emphasis in four main ways:

- to draw special attention to a noun or other pronoun. This is particularly common to emphasise the subject of the verb:

Moi, je pense que. . .	*I think that. . .*
Elle, elle sort souvent, mais **lui, il** reste à la maison.	*She often goes out, but he stays at home.*

As you can see, we don't normally need to use this sort of emphatic pronoun in English.

- in a short phrase (question, answer, exclamation) without a verb:

Qui a cassé ce verre? **Toi**?	*Who broke this glass? You?*

- after a preposition:

Il travaille **sans moi**.	*He works without me.*
Je vais arriver après **vous**.	*I'm going to arrive after you.*

But when you want to say *to him/to her/to it/to them*, you must normally use the indirect object pronoun (see pages 40–41) or **y** (see pages 42–43).

■ *à* **with emphatic pronouns**
One important exception where you *do* use **à** + the emphatic pronoun is the idiomatic expression **être à quelqu'un** = *to belong to someone*:

Cette valise est à **vous**? Non, elle est à **eux**.	*Does this case belong to you? No, it's theirs.*

• when you want to say *it's me, it was them*, etc.

Bonjour, c'est **moi**, Aline.	*Hello, it's me, Aline.*
Qui était à la porte? C'étaient **eux**.	*Who was at the door? It was them.*

■ *C'est/ce sont* + **emphatic pronouns**
Note the expression **C'est/Ce sont** + emphatic pronoun + **qui/que** . . ., which means *X is the one/They are the ones who . . .*:

C'est elle qui l'a choisi.	*She's the one who chose it.*
C'étaient eux que j'ai remarqués.	*They were the ones I noticed.*

▼ Activity 8   *Pronouns used for emphasis*

Choose the right emphatic pronoun to translate the word in brackets.

a   Il y a quelqu'un à la porte. C'est (her).
b   Je n'aurais pas pu le faire sans (them).
c   C'est (him) qui fait le pain? Non, c'est (me).
d   Tu l'achètes pour qui? Pour (us)?
e   Ce classeur est à (you) ou à (her)?
f   Allez, les enfants! On va partir sans (you)!
g   Marie et Claudine, (they) ont besoin de (him).
h   Christine et André? Ce sont (them) qui te l'ont dit?

▼ Mine, yours, etc. – possessive pronouns

A possessive pronoun (*mine, yours,* etc.) replaces the noun (person, place, thing) in phrases like *my watch, your parents, his friends, her designs.*

C'est ma montre. C'est **la mienne**.	*It's my watch. It's mine.*
Ce sont tes timbres. Ce sont **les tiens**.	*They're your stamps. They're yours.*

In French, the possessive pronoun consists of two words: **le, la, les + mien, tien,** etc. The **mien, tien** part is like an adjective, so you must make it singular or plural, masculine or feminine to agree with the noun it refers to.

Remember! it agrees with the noun which is owned, *not* with the owner:

Ce sont tes gants, Marie-Sophie? Oui, ce sont **les miens**.	*Are these your gloves, Sophie? Yes, they're mine.*

Tes gants are masculine plural.

J'ai oublié ma clé. Tu peux me donner **la tienne**, Didier?	*I've forgotten my key. Can you give me yours, Didier?*

Ma clé is feminine singular.

Here are all the possessive pronouns. Each one has four forms:

Mon chien = *my dog* (masc. sing.) le mien = *mine*

Ma maison = *my house* (fem. sing.) la mienne = *mine*

Mes pieds = *my feet* (masc. plural) les miens = *mine*

Mes idées = *my ideas* (fem. plural) les miennes = *mine*

masc. sing.	fem. sing.	masc. pl. or mixed masc/ fem. pl.	fem. pl.	Meaning
le mien	la mienne	les miens	les miennes	*mine*
le tien	la tienne	les tiens	les tiennes	*yours*
le sien	la sienne	les siens	les siennes	*his, hers, its, one's*
le nôtre	la nôtre	les nôtres	les nôtres	*ours*
le vôtre	la vôtre	les vôtres	les vôtres	*yours*
le leur	la leur	les leurs	les leurs	*theirs*

Question: If **le sien, la sienne**, etc. can mean both *his* and *hers*, isn't it very confusing?

Answer: Not really! You use **le sien, la sienne,** etc. when from the context you know whether it will mean *his* or *hers*:

Ce livre appartient à Yvonne? Oui, c'est **le sien**.	*Does this book belong to Yvonne? Yes, it's **hers**.*

But if the context doesn't make it clear, then you can use **à lui** (= *his*) or **à elle** (= *hers*):

Ces papiers sont **à lui** ou **à elle**?	*Are these papers his or hers?*

If you need to make *his* or *hers* the subject or object of the sentence, you can repeat the noun with **à lui** or **à elle**:

Sa chambre à lui est bleue, mais **sa chambre à elle** est jaune.	*His room is blue, but hers/her room is yellow.*

■ **Etre à + emphatic pronoun**

Another common way of saying *mine, yours,* etc. is to use the expression **être à** + *emphatic pronoun*:

Les CD qui sont **à moi** sont à gauche.	*The CDs which are mine are on the left.*
Ces boîtes sont **à nous**.	*These boxes are ours.*

▼ Activity 9   *Possessive pronouns*

Use a possessive pronoun to replace the underlined words.

a   Ces papiers sont <u>à toi</u>?
b   La moto toute neuve est <u>à vous</u>?
c   Regarde la photo. Cette maison est <u>à eux</u>, celle-ci est <u>à nous</u>.
d   Michel a acheté cette voiture? Oui, elle est <u>à lui</u>.
e   Est-ce que cet imperméable appartient à Carine? Non, ce n'est pas <u>à elle</u>.
f   Attends, ces bouteilles ne sont pas <u>à nous</u>!
g   Ah, je me suis trompé de clés! Celles-ci sont <u>à eux</u> peut-être?
h   Cet appartement n'est plus <u>à elle</u>.
i   Ces chaussettes ne sont pas <u>à moi</u>.

▼ This, that, these, those – demonstrative pronouns

There are two kinds of demonstrative pronouns.

▼ *Ce, ça, ceci, cela*

These general demonstrative pronouns mean *it*, *this* and *that*. They can be used as the subject or object of a verb, or after a preposition:

C'est mon frère.	*It's my brother.*
Il n'aime pas cela.	*He doesn't like that.*

Ce is used as the subject of **être**. Use one of **ceci**, **cela** or **ça** as the subject of any other verb:

Ce sont les nouvelles chaises.	*It's/They're the new chairs.*
Ceci/Cela/Ça semble difficile.	*This/That/It seems difficult.*

Question: What's the difference between **ceci** and **cela**?
Answer: Usually **ceci** means *this* and **cela** means *that*, but the French tend to use **cela** a lot more than **ceci**.

In spoken French **ça** (a short form of **cela**) is used a lot. Think of:

Ça va?	*How are you? How are things?*
Ça fait combien?	*How much is it?/How much does it cost?*

You can use **ça** instead of **cela** when you're writing to friends, leaving a note, and so on, but if you need to write something more formal (a letter to a hotel or an essay), it's better to use **cela**.

▼ *Celui, celle, ceux, celles*

These demonstrative pronouns have the basic meaning *this one/that one/these ones/the one(s)*. They are used to avoid repeating **ce/cet/cette/ces** + noun:

Elle aime ce parfum, mais elle n'aime pas celui qu'on vend chez Magritte.	*She likes this perfume, but she doesn't like **that one/the one** they sell at Magritte's.*

Celui = ce parfum

You must choose the form of **celui** to agree (singular or plural, masculine or feminine) with the noun you are replacing:

Ce garçon = celui (masc. singular)
Cette fille = celle (fem. singular)
Ces hommes = ceux (masc. plural)
Ces femmes = celles (fem. plural)

Celui, **celle**, etc. are always used in one of these three ways:

• followed by **-ci** or **-là**, to distinguish between *this one* and *that one*:

Vous voulez des chocolats?	*Do you want some chocolates?*
Oui, mais pas **ceux-ci**, je préfère **ceux-là**.	*Yes, but not these ones, I prefer those ones.*

-**ci** is the one nearest to you, -**là** the one furthest away.

■ **The former, the latter**

In written French you will often meet **celui-là** = *the first one mentioned*, the former, in contrast to **celui-ci** = *the last one mentioned*, the latter:

Le président a rencontré le premier ministre britannique et le roi espagnol. Celui-ci est arrivé ce matin, celui-là hier soir.	*The President met the British Prime Minister and the Spanish king. The latter (the Spanish king) arrived this morning, the former (the British Prime Minister) yesterday evening.*

• followed by **de** + *noun*, meaning *the one belonging to*:

Nous avons deux voitures. **Celle de** mon père est rouge, **celle de** ma mère est noire.	*We have two cars. The one belonging to my father/My father's is red, the one belonging to my mother/my mother's is black.*

You can see from this example that we often translate **celui de** by the form *X's* in English:

Cet album est **celui de** ma grand-mère. *This album is my grandmother's.*

Remember that you must always choose the form of **celui** to agree (singular or plural, masculine or feminine) with the noun which is owned, *not* the owner!

- followed **qui/que/dont** (or other relative pronoun – see pages 56–57), meaning *the one who/the one which/the one that/the one whose/the one of which*:

La femme qui entre dans le magasin est **celle qui** a acheté notre maison.	*The woman going into the shop is the one who bought our house.*
Vous allez lire quels livres?	*Which books are you going to read?*
Ceux que j'ai achetés hier.	*The ones that I bought yesterday.*

Question: In English we often say just *the one* and leave out *who/which/that*. Can I do the same in French?
Answer: No. You must always use celui **qui/que/dont** in French, even when English leaves out *who, which, that*:

J'avais deux lapins. **Celui que** j'ai perdu s'appelait 'Carottes'.	*I had two rabbits. The one I lost was called 'Carrots'.*

▼ Activity 10   *Demonstrative pronouns*

Choose the correct form *celui/celle/ceux/celles* to complete each of the gaps. The words in the box below will help you.

- Bonjour Madame, Vous regardez ces nouveaux parapluies?
- Oui, ...-là fait combien?
- 180 francs, Madame.
- Oh là là! Ils sont tous aussi chers?
- Non, les plus petits, – . . . .-ci, sont à 90 francs.
- Non, je crois que je vais essayer des chaussures: . . . .-ci.
- Bien sûr, Madame.
- Non, attendez, je préfère un autre modèle, ...-là.
- Ces chaussures-ci, les rouges?
- Non, ...-là, les bleues. Elles iront très bien avec mon sac – ah, non, pas . . . .-ci, l'autre que j'ai à la maison.
- Voilà, Madame, vous voulez vous asseoir sur cette chaise?
- Ah, non! . . . .-ci est sale!
- Je suis désolé, alors prenez . . . .-là. Vous faites quelle pointure?
- Ah, ça dépend du pied! . . . .-ci fait du 35 mais . . . .-là fait du 37.
- Mais comment faites-vous alors?
- D'habitude je vais dans un autre magasin, plus grand que . . . .-ci.
- Alors, Madame, je vous conseille d'y retourner!

le parapluie	la chaussure	le modèle	le sac	la chaise
le magasin	la pointure			

▼ Someone, something, each one, etc. – indefinite pronouns

Indefinite pronouns can refer to people, places or things. Here is a list of the most common ones:

- in positive sentences:

quelqu'un = *someone*
Il y a quelqu'un à la porte.   *There's someone at the door.*

quelque chose = *something*
Il m'a donné quelque chose.   *He gave me something.*

l'une . . . l'autre (+ singular verb) = *the one . . . the other*
Il y a deux portes. L'une est fermée,   *There are two doors. One's shut,*
l'autre est ouverte.   *the other's open.*

les un(s) . . . les autres (+ plural verb) = *some . . . others*
Quant aux étudiants, les uns iront   *As for the students, some will go*
en France, les autres en Espagne.   *to France, the others to Spain.*

chacun, chacune = *each one, everyone*
Ces livres coûtent 100F chacun.   *These books cost 100 francs each.*

tous, toutes (+ plural verb) = *all*, *everyone*
Ils sont tous partis.   *Everyone has left./All have left.*

tout (+ singular verb) = *everything, all*
Tout est perdu!   *Everything is lost!/All is lost!*

on = *someone, people, you, we* (see page 38).
On ne peut rien faire sans lui.   *One/People/You/We can't do*
     anything without him.

plusieurs = *several, some, a few*
Il en veut plusieurs.   *He wants several of them.*

n'importe qui (+ singular verb) = *anyone*
N'importe qui peut te donner son   *Anyone can give you his/her*
adresse.   *address.*

n'importe quoi (+ singular verb) = *anything*
Il mange n'importe quoi.   *He eats anything.*

n'importe où = *anywhere*
Elle est prête à aller n'importe où.   *She's ready to go anywhere.*

n'importe quand = *at any time*
Vous pouvez me téléphoner   *You can phone me at any time.*
n'importe quand.

■ **Someone interesting, something old**

When you want to say *someone interesting, something old*, etc.
you need to use:

quelqu'un de + adjective in the masculine singular
quelque chose de + adjective in the masculine singular

J'ai recontré **quelqu'un d'**intéressant hier.	*I met someone interesting yesterday.*
J'ai besoin de **quelque chose de** nouveau.	*I need something new.*

• in negative sentences (see pages 124–25 also):

personne = *no one*
Personne n'a répondu.	*Nobody answered.*

rien = *nothing*
Le médecin n'a rien vu.	*The doctor saw nothing.*

pas grand-chose = *not much.*
Il n'y a pas grand-chose à te dire.	*There's not much to tell you.*

You can see from these examples that you need **ne** before the
verb when you use these negative pronouns. You could think of
them as replacing the **pas** in ne . . . **pas**.

Je **n'**ai **pas** d'argent.	*I have no money.*
Je **n'**ai **rien**.	*I have nothing.*

■ **Nothing + adjective**

When you want to say *nothing interesting, nothing old*, etc. you
need to use:

rien de + adjective in the masculine singular

Il n'y a **rien d'**intéressant à voir.	*There's nothing interesting to see.*

▼ Activity 11   *Indefinite pronouns*

Choose one of these indefinite pronouns to fill in each gap: *on,
pas grand-chose, personne, quelque chose, quelqu'un, rien.*

Un cadeau perdu
J'oublie toujours mes affaires. Hier je venais d'acheter . . . . pour
l'anniversaire de ma petite amie, ... de très cher, mais ça devait lui
faire plaisir. Quand je suis descendu du bus j'ai oublié mon sac.
Heureusement que . . . . l'a remarqué . . . . a essayé de m'appeler, mais
je n'entendais . . . . avec toute la circulation. Ce matin, je ne
faisais . . . . , je lisais un magazine, quand le téléphone a sonné.
D'abord je croyais que c'était la porte. Je suis allé l'ouvrir, mais il n'y
avait . . . . . Puis j'ai répondu au téléphone, et . . . . m'a dit que . . . .
avait trouvé mon sac. Le problème, c'est que . . . . ne peut me dire où
se trouve le bureau des objets trouvés!

▼ Who, which, that, whose, etc. – relative pronouns

Words like *who*, *which*, *that*, *whose* are relative pronouns. They
'relate' to a noun or an idea expressed earlier in the sentence:

La fille **que** j'ai vue s'appelle Marie. | *The girl **that** I saw is called Marie.*
La maison **dont** tu parles a été vendue. | *The house **which** you're talking about has been sold.*

In English we could miss out the relative pronouns *that* and *which*
in these examples, but in French you must always put in the
relative pronoun, even when it is not there in English:

Voici le tire-bouchon **que** j'ai trouvé. | *Here's the corkscrew I found.*

The most common relative pronouns in French are:

qui = *who, which, that*
que = *who, whom, which, that*
où = *where, in which*

La secrétaire **qui** travaille avec Madame Dupont est très gentille. | *The secretary who works with Madame Dupont is very kind.*
Le film **que** tu vas voir a été tourné à Quimper. | *The film (that) you're going to see was shot in Quimper.*
Le quartier **où** j'habite a deux jardins publics. | *The area where I live has two parks.*

Question: **qui** and **que** seem to mean the same, so how do I know which to use?

Answer: It *is* important to choose the right one. **Qui** is the subject of the next verb (which means it is usually followed immediately by the verb):

Voici la personne **qui** peut vous aider.	*Here's the person who can help you.*

SUBJECT   VERB

Que is the object of the next verb in the sentence. There is usually another noun or pronoun – the subject – between **que** and the next verb:

Voici les   lettres **que**   **j'**   ai reçues.

OBJECT   SUBJECT   VERB

■ When to use *où*

As well as meaning *where*, referring to a place, **où** is used to say *when* after a noun talking about a time or period:

Le jour **où** je suis rentré, il a commencé à neiger.	*The day **when** I came back, it started to snow.*
A l'époque **où** nous habitions à la campagne, il n'y avait pas d'industrie ici.	*At the time **when** we lived in the country there was no industry here.*

But watch out for one common exception:

Un jour que je me promenais dans le bois . . .	*One day when I was going for a walk in the woods . . .*

You will also meet some other relative pronouns:

- **dont** = *whose, of whom, of which*

C'est notre voisin **dont** tu connais déjà le fils.	*It's our neighbour whose son you already know.*
C'est le même sujet dont nous parlions.	*It's the same subject (that) we were speaking of.* (literally: *of which we were speaking*)

• **ce qui, ce que** = (1) *what*

Je ne sais pas **ce qui** se passe	I don't know what's happening.
Il m'a demandé **ce que** je faisais.	He asked me what I was doing.

• **ce qui, ce que** = (2) *which* (referring back not to just one noun, but the rest of the sentence):

Nous allons à Beaulieu, **ce qui** amuse les enfants.	We're going to Beaulieu, which is fun for the children.
(**ce qui** = the fact that we are going to Beaulieu)	
Il a fumé dans la cuisine, **ce que** je déteste.	He smoked in the kitchen, which I hate.
(**ce que** = the fact that he smoked in the kitchen)	

Question: **ce qui** and **ce que** seem to mean the same, so how do I know which to use?

Answer: It *is* important to choose the right one. **Ce qui** is the subject of the next verb (which means it is usually followed immediately by the verb):

Voici	ce qui	intéresse mon père. *Here's what interests my father.*
	SUBJECT VERB	

Ce que is the object of the next verb (which means there is usually another noun or pronoun – as the subject – between **ce que** and the next verb):

Il voulait savoir	ce que	nous	en pensions. *He wanted to know*
	OBJECT	SUBJECT	VERB *what we thought of it.*

• **lequel, laquelle, lesquels, lesquelles** = *who, whom, which, that*
  Lequel, laquelle, etc., are used mainly when you are talking about things and need a *preposition* + *which, that*. You need to choose the form of **lequel, laquelle**, etc. to agree (masculine or feminine, singular or plural) with the noun you are referring back to:

Voici le château devant **lequel** nous avons pique-niqué.	Here's the castle in front of which we had a picnic, or Here's the castle we had a picnic in front of.

Ce sont les couleurs avec **lesquelles** nous avons travaillé.	*These are the colours with which we worked,* or *These are the colours we worked with.*

▼ Activity 12   *Relative pronouns*

Fill in the gaps in the sentences below with one of these pronouns: *qui, que, où, ce qui, ce que.*

a   Je ne comprends pas . . . . tu dis.

b   Voici l'endroit . . . . nous avons tourné le film.

c   J'ai un chat . . . . j'aime beaucoup.

d   Il m'a demandé . . . . se passe.

e   C'est elle . . . . doit commencer?

f   Comment s'appelle le restaurant . . . . nous avons mangé à midi?

g   Le vélo . . . . Charles a acheté coûtait 1200 francs!

h   Je veux savoir . . . . vous allez faire maintenant.

▼▼▼
PREPOSITIONS
position and relation of things

Prepositions are words which go before nouns or verbs. Many prepositions indicate position (*in*, *at*, *from*, etc.) or time (*before*, *during*, *after*):

Le vin est **dans** la cave.	*The wine is in the cellar.*
Tu peux me téléphoner **avant de** partir.	*You can phone me before leaving.*

The main problem with the prepositions in a foreign language is learning phrases which use a different preposition from English, e.g.

par example	*for example* (**par** literally means *by*)
Je suis **de** retour.	*I'm back.* (**de retour** literally means *of return*)

The sections below indicate some of the most common idiomatic expressions using different prepositions, but of course you will meet others as you read or listen to more French.

▼ Prepositions used before verbs

▼ *Prepositions used before an infinitive*
When you have a first verb followed by another verb in the infinitive, sometimes you need a preposition between the two verbs. The three prepositions which can be used in this way are **à**, **de**, **par**:

Vous avez commencé **à** les préparer?	*Have you started to prepare them?*
Elle a décidé **de** l'épouser.	*She's decided to marry him.*
J'ai fini **par** l'acheter.	*I ended up buying it.*

You do need to learn the most common structures, but if you are stuck, as a rule of thumb, the majority of verbs are followed by **de**. However, in some cases – e.g. **vouloir** + *infinitive*, **espérer** + *infinitive* – the first verb does not require any preposition before the verb in the infinitive:

Tu **veux prendre** mon vélo?	*Do you want to take my bike?*
Ils **espèrent rentrer** avant six heures.	*They hope to get back before six o'clock.*

The lists below give you the structure to use after the most common verbs + *infinitive*.

▼ Common verbs followed by the infinitive with no preposition

adorer = *to love to*
aimer = *to like to*
aimer mieux = *to prefer to*
aller = *to go to/to go and/to be going to*
désirer = *to wish to, want to*
détester = *to hate to*
devoir = *to have to, must do*
écouter = *to listen to (something happening)*
entendre = *to hear (something happening)*
espérer = *to hope to*
faire = *to have/get (something done)*
falloir (il faut) = *to be necessary to, to have to*
laisser = *to have/let (something be done)*
oser = *to dare to*
paraître = *to seem to*
penser = *to plan to*
pouvoir = *to be able to/can do*
préférer = *to prefer to*
regarder = *to look at/watch (something happening)*
savoir = *to know how to/be able to*
valoir mieux = *to be better to*
venir = *to come to/come and*
voir = *to see (something happening)*
vouloir = *to want to*

Vous **voulez aller** au cinéma ou vous **aimez mieux rester** à la maison?	*Do you want to go to the cinema or would you prefer to stay at home?*
Si tu **dois me téléphoner**, il **vaut mieux essayer** après huit heures du soir.	*If you have to phone me, it's better to try after 8 p.m.*
Venez nous voir quand vous voulez.	*Come and see us when you want.*

Question: If **pouvoir** and **savoir** both mean *to be able to*, what's the difference between them?

Answer: **Pouvoir** is used to talk about something you are physically able to do, and **savoir** for something you have learned how to do:

Tu sais nager?	*Can you swim? (Have you learned how to?)*
Je ne peux pas nager aujourd'hui parce que je me suis fait mal au bras.	*I can't swim today because I've hurt my arm. (I can't = I'm physically unable).*

Several other common expressions use **savoir +** *infinitive* to translate *can*:

Vous savez **conduire**?	*Can you drive?*
Tu sais **parler** italien?	*Can you speak Italian?*
Ta petite soeur sait **lire et écrire**?	*Can your little sister read and write?*
Je sais **jouer au** tennis.	*Can you play tennis?*
Elle sait **jouer de la** guitare.	*She can play the guitar.*

■ **To see, hear, etc. something happening**

To translate expressions like *to see, hear, watch, listen to something happening* you need to use **voir/entendre, regarder/écouter +** the *infinitive* of the next verb:

J'ai **vu** les garçons **traverser** la rue.	*I saw the boys crossing the road.*
Elle a **entendu** le chien **aboyer**.	*She heard the dog barking.*

▼ **Activity 1**   *To see, hear, etc. something happening*

Translate the words in brackets into French:

a Dis-moi si tu vois (a lorry arriving).
b Tu as entendu (a child crying)?
c Elle écoutait (her son talking).
d Vous allez voir (the boys jumping off the wall).
e Je vais regarder (Gisèle swimming).
f Nous t'entendions (playing the guitar).
g Mon père a entendu (someone breaking the window).
h Tu as vu (the girls playing tennis)?

■ To have/get something done

To translate the expressions *to have/get something done* you need to use the verb **faire +** the *infinitive* of the next verb:

Nous avons **fait réparer** le lave-vaisselle.	*We got/had the dishwasher repaired.*
Tu dois **te faire couper** les cheveux.	*You must get your hair cut.*

You can see from these examples that in French the thing which you have/get done (i.e. the object of the infinitive), goes *after* the infinitive.

There are several very common idiomatic expressions with **faire +** *infinitive*:

faire voir quelque chose = *to show something*

Elle m'a fait voir le jardin.	*She showed me the garden.*
Fais voir!/Faites voir!	*Show me!/Let me see!*

faire venir quelqu'un = *to call someone out/get someone to come*

To devras faire venir le médecin.	*You'll have to get the doctor to come.*

se faire avoir = *to be caught/to be caught out, to be done*

Il ne m'ont pas rendu la monnaie. Je me suis fait avoir!	*They didn't give me back the change. I've been done/caught out!*
Attention! Le concierge arrive! Tu vas te faire avoir!	*Watch out, the caretaker's coming! You're going to be caught.*

■ To have something to do

One very common expression using **à +** the *infinitive* is:
avoir quelque chose à faire = *to have something to do*

J'ai des lettres à écrire.	*I've got some letters to write.*
Vous avez des courses à faire?	*Have you got some shopping to do?*

▼ Activity 2   Faire + *infinitive*

Put these sentences in the right gaps below to complete the conversation:

a   Tu le feras changer?
b   Alors il faudra faire venir le garagiste.
c   Tu vas te faire avoir!
d   Tu devras la faire réparer.
e   Attends. Fais voir.

Une panne

–   J'ai un problème avec la voiture.
–   (1) ....
–   Mais elle ne démarre pas du tout.
–   (2) ....
–   C'est peut-être le moteur!
–   (3) ....
–   Non, ça coûte trop cher. Mais ça pourrait être quelque chose d'autre peut-être . . .
–   (4) .... Mais tu n'as plus d'essence!
–   Oh là, là! Ah, zut! Maintenant il y a un agent de police qui arrive – et je n'ai pas le droit de me garer ici en plus!
–   (5) ....

▼ *Common verbs followed by* à + *the infinitive*

aider (quelqu'un) à = *to help (someone) to*
s'amuser à = *to have fun, a good time (doing something)*
apprendre à = *to learn (how) to*
apprendre (à quelqu'un) à = *to teach (someone) how to*
arriver à = *to manage to*
avoir (quelque chose) à faire = *to have something to do*
chercher à = *to try to*
commencer à = *to start/begin to*
continuer à = *to carry on/continue (doing something)*
se décider à = *to make up one's mind to*
encourager (quelqu'un) à = *to encourage (someone) to*
s'habituer à = *to get used to*
inviter (quelqu'un) à = *to invite someone to*
se mettre à = *to start/begin to*
obliger (quelqu'un) à = *to force (someone) to/make (someone do something)*
passer (une heure, etc.) à = *to spend (an hour, etc.) doing*

renoncer à = *to give up (doing)*
réussir à = *to succeed in (doing)/to manage to*

Quand est-ce que tu **as appris à dessiner**?	*When did you learn to draw?*
Elle **a invité** sa copine à **rester** chez elle.	*She invited her friend to stay at her house.*
Nous **avons passé** tout l'après-midi à **jouer** avec le chien.	*We spent the whole afternoon playing with the dog.*

■ To be done, etc.

The expression '**être à** + *infinitive*' is used as follows:

Cette boîte **est à jeter** dans la poubelle.	*This box is to be thrown in the dustbin.*
Cette maison **est à vendre**.	*This house is to be sold/for sale.*

You may see notices based on this expression, using **à** + *infinitive*:

A emporter = *Take away* (i.e. to be taken away)
A louer = *For hire* (i.e. to be hired)
A vendre = *For sale* (i.e. to be sold)

▼ Common verbs followed by de + the infinitive

s'agir de (il s'agit de) = *it's a question/matter of (doing)*
avoir peur de = *to be afraid of (doing)*
choisir de = *to choose to*
décider de = *to decide to*
empêcher (quelqu'un) de = *to stop someone from (doing)*
essayer de = *to try to*
éviter de = *to avoid (doing)*
faire semblant de = *to pretend to*
finir de = *to finish (doing)*
manquer de = *to fail/forget to*
ne pas manquer de = *to be sure to*
oublier de = *to forget to*
refuser de = *to refuse to*
regretter de = *to be sorry to*
remercier (quelqu'un) de = *to thank someone (for doing)*
risquer de = *to risk (doing)*
venir de = *to have just (done)**

* See explanation on the following page.

Vous voulez **essayer de le tenir**?   *Do you want to try to hold it?*
Tu ne dois **pas manquer de voir**   *You must be sure to see my father.*
mon père.
Je **regrette de vous déranger**,   *I'm sorry to disturb you, but . . .*
mais . . .

■ To have just done

The expression **venir de** + *infinitive* is used to translate
have/has just done and *had just done*:
    To say . . . *has/have just done*, use the ***present*** tense of **venir**
+ de + *infinitive*:

Je viens d'arriver.   *I have just arrived.*
Elle vient de manger.   *She has just eaten.*

To say . . . *had just done*, use the ***imperfect*** tense of **venir + de**
+ *infinitive*:

Ils venaient de voir le film.   *They had just seen the film.*
Nous venions de sortir.   *We had just gone out.*

■ Il est/c'est . . . de . . .

To say *It is* **+** *adjective to* (do something), you need to use
Il est/c'est **+** *adjective* **de** (faire quelque chose):

Il est/c'est difficile de décider.   *It's difficult to decide.*
Il est/c'est impossible de le   *It's impossible to contact him.*
contacter.

You'll find **il est** is more common in formal written French, but
c'est is often used in spoken French.

▼ Activity 3   *Il est/c'est . . . de . . .*

Put these sentences in the right gaps below to complete the conversation:

a Il est impossible de rien entendre avec tous les jeunes qui mangent du pop-corn.
b Il est triste de rester tout le temps à la maison.
c Il est trop compliqué d'organiser un rendez-vous.
d Mais il est difficile de trouver un bon livre.
e Il est sûr de pleuvoir.

Le pessimiste

– Vous allez à la mer ce weekend?
– Non. (1) ....
– Vous restez chez vous alors? Qu'est-ce que vous allez faire?
– J'aimerais lire. (2) ....
– Vous allez au cinéma peut-être?
– Non. (3) ....
– Et vous n'aimeriez pas sortir avec des amis?
– Non. (4) ....
– Vous aimez être seul donc?
– Pas du tout! (5) .... Mais personne ne m'invite jamais. Je me demande pourquoi . . .

▼ Common verbs followed by à + *person* + de + *the infinitive*

An important group of verbs to do with *telling someone to do something*, *asking someone to do something* etc. all require the structure *verb* **à** + **quelqu'un de** + *infinitive*:

conseiller à quelqu'un de = *to advise someone to*
défendre à quelqu'un de = *to forbid someone to*
demander à quelqu'un de = *to ask someone to*
dire à quelqu'un de = *to tell someone to*
interdire à quelqu'un de = *to forbid someone to*
offrir à quelqu'un de = *to offer someone to*
ordonner à quelqu'un de = *to order someone to*
permettre à quelqu'un de = *to allow someone to*
promettre à quelqu'un de = *to promise someone to*
proposer à quelqu'un de = *to suggest to someone to*

J'ai demandé à mon frère de me rendre mon dictionnaire.
    I asked my brother to give me back my dictionary.

Le directeur **a interdit à tous les élèves de marcher** sur la pelouse.	*The headmaster has forbidden all the pupils to walk on the grass.*
Elle **a promis à ma mère de ramener** du parfum.	*She promised my mother to bring back some perfume.*

Remember that if you replace **à quelqu'un** by a pronoun after these verbs you will need the **indirect** object pronoun (see pages 40–41):

J'ai conseillé **au journaliste** d'attendre.	*I advised the journalist to wait.*
Je **lui** ai conseillé d'attendre.	*I advised him to wait.*

■ . . . is forbidden

For . . . *is forbidden* you will meet the expression **défense de** + infinitive:

Défense de fumer.	*Smoking is forbidden./No smoking*
Défense de se baigner.	*Bathing is forbidden./No bathing*

Alternatively, in some cases you will find *noun* + **interdit**:

Stationnement interdit.	*Parking is forbidden./No parking*

▼ *Common verbs followed by* **par** + *the infinitive*

There are only three common verbs followed by **par** + the infinitive:

commencer par = *to start/begin by*
continuer par = *to continue/carry on by*
finir par = *to finish by*

Je vais **commencer par vous raconter** une histoire.	*I'm going to start by telling you a story.*
Il **a fini par tout casser**.	*He ended up breaking everything.*

▼ *After doing/after having done*

To say *after doing/after having done* . . . you need to use the expression **après avoir** + *past participle* or **après être** + *past participle*:

Après avoir signé le contrat, nous avons bu du champagne.	*After signing the contract, we drank champagne.*

| Après être allés à Lourdes, ils se sentaient mieux. | *After going to Lourdes, they felt better.* |

Question: How do I know whether to use **après avoir** or **après être?**

Answer: Use **après avoir** if you are using a verb which makes the perfect tense with **avoir** (see page 97):

| Après avoir fait son lit, elle a pris son petit déjeuner. | *After making the bed, she had her breakfast.* |

Use **après être** if the verb makes the perfect tense with **être** (many verbs of motion and all reflexive verbs – see pages 97–98):

| Après s'être couchée, elle a lu pendant une demi-heure. | *After going to bed, she read for half an hour.* |

(For the agreement of the past participle in these structures, see pages 101–103).

Note: You cannot use **après avoir/être + past participle** if the subject of this verb is different from the subject of the next verb: e.g. *After she smiled, he sat down.* In this case you need to use **après que +** *conjugated verb.*

▼ *Before doing*
To say *before doing*, you need to use the expression **avant de +** *infinitive:*

| Avant de répondre, Louis a regardé sa montre. | *Before answering, Louis looked at his watch.* |
| Elle nous dira au revoir avant de partir. | *She'll say goodbye to us before leaving/before she leaves.* |

Note: You cannot use **avant de +** *infinitive* if the subject of this verb is different from the subject of the next verb: e.g. *I phoned them before my boss set out.* In this case you need to use **avant que + *subjunctive*** (see page 112).

▼ Activity 4   Après avoir/après être + *past participle*; avant de + *infinitive*

Make one sentence from the pairs of sentences using *après avoir/ après être* for (a)–(d) and *avant de* for (e)–(h):

Example:
Il a téléphoné à son ami. Puis il est sorti.
Après avoir téléphoné à son ami, il est sorti.
Il a téléphoné à son ami avant de sortir.

a   Elle a pris une douche. Puis elle a mis un nouveau pantalon.
b   Charles et Patricia ont trouvé un parking. Puis ils ont visité la ville.
c   Mon grand-père s'est reposé. Puis il a fait du jardinage.
d   Madame Lebrun a fait ses courses. Puis elle est allée chez son amie.

e   J'ai mis ma montre. Puis je me suis levé.
f   Manon a caché le cadeau. Puis elle est sortie dans le jardin.
g   Nous nous sommes baignés. Puis nous avons mangé les gâteaux.
h   Ils sont allés à la poste. Puis ils se sont promenés en ville.

▼ To do/in order to do

To say *(in order) to do something* use the expression **pour +** *infinitive*:

Je suis passé par Le Mans **pour éviter** les bouchons.	*I went through Le Mans to avoid the traffic jams.*
Tu devras regarder dans l'annuaire **pour trouver** le numéro.	*You'll have to look in the telephone directory to find the number.*

Note: You cannot use **pour +** *infinitive* if the subject of the infinitive is different from the subject of the next verb: e.g. *We bought the computer for my children to use it.* In this case you need to use **pour que +** *subjunctive*. (See page 112.)

▼ Without doing

To say *without doing something*, use **sans +** *infinitive*:

Ils sont partis **sans payer**.	*They left without paying.*
Vous allez arriver **sans leur téléphoner**?	*Are you going to turn up without phoning them?*

Note: You cannot use **sans** + *infinitive* if the subject of the infinitive is different from the subject of the next verb: e.g. *He left without Mary knowing*. In this case you need to use **sans que** + *subjunctive*. (See page 112.)

▼ While doing/by doing
En is the only preposition which is *not* followed by the infinitive. To say *while doing something* or *by doing something*, use the expression **en** + *present participle*. (For the form of the present participle, see page 118.)

Il fait ses devoirs **en écoutant** la radio.	He does his homework while listening to the radio.
Il a pu se payer des vacances **en travaillant** tous les weekends.	He managed to pay for his holidays by working every weekend.

If you want to stress the fact that someone is doing two things at the same time you can use **tout en** + *present participle*:

Je peux t'écouter tout en préparant le souper.	I can listen to you at the same time as I'm getting supper ready.

Note: You cannot use **en** + *present participle* if the subject of the participle is different from the subject of the next verb, e.g. *I have supper while my mum watches the news*. In this case, you need to use **pendant que** + *conjugated verb*.

▼ Activity 5   *While doing/by doing*

Translate the words in brackets into French:

a Tu peux regarder les magazines (while you're waiting).
b (While I was looking at the photo) j'ai remarqué que je connaissais la femme.
c Il a aidé les enfants (at the same time as he was talking to my uncle).
d Nous avons pu le retrouver (by looking in the garage).
e (While she was crossing the road) elle a perdu un gant.
f J'ai pu me payer le vélo (by washing cars).

▼ Prepositions used before nouns

This section gives a list of all the common prepositions with (a)
their literal meanings and (b) some of the most important
idiomatic expressions in which they are used. For prepositions
used with names of places, countries, etc. see pages 142–43.

▼ *à = to/at*

Remember that when you want to say *to the . . ./at the . . .* you
will need to use the forms **au, à l', à la, aux**. (See page 2.)

Ce train va à Bordeaux.	*This train goes to Bordeaux.*
J'ai trouvé ce sac au centre commercial.	*I found this bag at the shopping centre.*

Here is a list of the most common idioms:

• **à** + *times* (of the clock):

à trois heures et demie	*at half past three*
à minuit	*at midnight*

• **à** + *definite article* translates *with* . . . for descriptions of people
or places:

la fille aux cheveux noirs	*the girl with black hair*
l'homme aux lunettes de soleil	*the man with sunglasses*
la chambre aux rideaux bleus	*the room with blue curtains*

• **à** translates *in* in the following expressions:

à mon avis	*in my opinion*
à la campagne	*in the country* (but **en** ville)
à la mode de (Christian Dior)	*in the style of . . .*
au printemps	*in the spring* (but **en** for other seasons)
au vingtième siècle	*in the twentieth century*

• **à** is used for some methods of transport (but see also **en** and
par):

à bicyclette	*by bike* (but **en** vélo)
à cheval	*on horseback*
à moto	*by motorbike*
à pied	*on foot*

- **à** is used to express what something is for, in common phrases like:

une boîte à lettres	*a letter box*
une machine à laver	*a washing machine*
un moulin à café	*a coffee-grinder*
une tasse à thé	*a tea cup (but une tasse **de** thé = a cup of tea)*
une canne à pêche	*a fishing rod*

- Note also:

à droite	*on the right*
à gauche	*on the left*
à la main	*by hand*
à grands pas	*with big steps/strides*
(lire) à haute voix	*(to read) out loud*
côte à côte	*side by side*
petit à petit	*little by little, gradually*
peu à peu	*little by little, gradually*

■ To belong to (someone)

To say *this belongs to . . . .* you can use the expression **être à . . .**:

| A qui sont ces affaires? | *Whose are these things?* |
| Les vêtements sont à Caroline. | *The clothes belong to Caroline.* |

■ à meaning *from* after certain verbs

In English we talk about *hiding things from . . ./stealing things from . . . .* In French, with verbs like these you need to translate *from* by **à**:

| Je vais cacher les chocolats à ma soeur! | *I'm going to hide the chocolates from my sister!* |
| Il avait volé l'argent à son père. | *He had stolen the money from his father.* |

Other verbs following this pattern include:

prendre quelque chose à quelqu'un	*to take something from someone*
acheter quelque chose à quelqu'un	*to buy something from someone*
emprunter quelque chose à quelqu'un	*to borrow something from someone*

▼ *après = after*

Vous pouvez arriver **après** huit heures.	*You can arrive after eight o'clock.*

▼ *avant = before*

Je ne peux rien faire **avant** le petit déjeuner.	*I can't do anything before breakfast.*

▼ *avec = with*

Sophie est partie en vacances **avec** sa tante.	*Sophie has gone on holiday with her aunt.*

▼ *chez = at (the house of)/to (the house of)*

Vous serez logé **chez** Madame Camus.	*You'll be staying at Mrs Camus's house.*
Nous irons directement **chez** Bernard.	*We'll go directly to Bernard's.*

Note: chez le boulanger *at the baker's*, etc.; aller chez le médecin *to go to the doctor's*.

chez nous = in our house/in our family/in our country
chez vous = *in your house/in your family/in your country*

▼ *contre = against*

Je n'ai rien **contre** ce projet.	*I've nothing against this project.*

Note also: être fâché contre quelqu'un *to be angry with someone*; se fâcher contre quelqu'un *to get angry with someone*

▼ *dans = in/into*

Quand vous entrez **dans** la cave, faites attention à la marche.	*When you go into the cellar, mind the step.*

• **dans** + *time = in . . . from now*

Dans trois semaines nous serons en vacances.	*In three weeks (from now) we'll be on holiday.*

▼ *de = of/from*

Remember that when you want to say *of the . . ./from the . . .* you will need to use the forms **du, de l', de la, des** (see page 4).

C'est le nom **de la** rue.	*It's the name of the road.*
Il vient **du** nord **de la** France.	*He comes from the north of France.*

Note also:

de ce côté	*on/from this side*
de cette façon	*in this way*
de cette manière	*in this way*
d'un pas (rapide)	*at a (quick) pace*
d'un ton fâché	*in a cross tone/voice*
être de retour	*to be back*
d'une voix (malheureuse)	*in an (unhappy) voice*

▼ *depuis = for, since*

Je ne les ai plus revus **depuis** Noel.	*I haven't seen them since Christmas.*
J'attends **depuis** vingt minutes.	*I've been waiting for twenty minutes.*

Note: for the verb tenses to use with **depuis** see pages 88 and 94–95.

▼ *derrière = behind*

Elle a mis la chaise derrière le piano.	*She's put the chair behind the piano.*

▼ *dès = from (a certain time)*

Dès la semaine prochaine j'aurai ma propre voiture.	*From next week I'll have my own car.*

▼ *devant = in front of*

Ne laisse pas ton vélo devant la porte!	*Don't leave your bike in front of the door!*

▼ *en = in*

Elle habite en Italie.	*She lives in Italy.*

Here is a list of idioms using **en**:

- **en** is used for some locations (see pages 142–43 for **en** + countries).

Note also:

en plein air = *outside/in the open air*
en ville = *in town* (*but* à la campagne = *in the country*)

- **en** is used for *in* (a language):

en anglais = *in English*   en français = *in French*

- with expression of time **en** = *within/in* (i.e. time taken to do something).

Avec le Tunnel sous la Manche on peut aller de Londres à Paris **en** trois heures.

With the Channel Tunnel you can get from London to Paris in three hours.

- **en** is also used in these other time expressions:

en hiver, en été, en automne = *in winter, in summer, in autumn*
(*but* au printemps)
en janvier, en février, etc. = *in January, in February, etc.*
en 1789, en 2010, etc. = *in (the year) 1789, 2010, etc.*

- **en** is used for many forms of transport (but see also **à** and **par**):

en avion = *by plane*
en bateau = *by boat* (*also* par le bateau)
en bus = *by bus* (*also* par le bus)
en car = *by coach/bus*
en train = *by train* (*also* par le train)
en vélo = *by bike* (*but* à bicyclette)
en voiture = *by car*

- In many cases **en** is used to say what things are made of:

un sac en plastique   *a plastic bag*
des chaussures en cuir   *leather shoes*

▼ *entre = between*

Vous devrez choisir **entre** les deux cafés.

You'll have to choose between the two cafés.

▼ *malgré* = *despite*

Ils se sont promenés **malgré** la chaleur.	*They went for a walk despite the heat.*

▼ *par* = *by/through*

Ce tableau a été fait **par** un enfant.	*This picture was done by a child.*

Here is a list of idioms using **par**:

* **par** is used to say how many times a day/a week, etc. you do something:

Je prends une douche deux fois **par** jour.	*I shower twice a day.*
Il y a un marché trois fois **par** semaine.	*There's a market three times a week.*

* **par** is used with words like **jour**, **journée**, **matin**, **matinée** to translate *on*:

par une belle journée ensoleillée	*on a fine sunny day*
par une nuit orageuse	*on a stormy night*

* **par** is also used in the following idioms:

par chance	*by a stroke of luck*
par conséquent	*consequently*
par écrit	*in writing*
par exemple	*for example*
(regarder) par la fenêtre	*(to look) out of the window*
par hasard	*by chance*
par terre	*on the ground*

▼ *parmi* = *among*

Il s'est caché **parmi** les arbres.	*He hid among the trees.*

▼ *pendant* = *during*

Qu'est-ce que tu as fait **pendant** l'après-midi?	*What did you do during the afternoon?*

▼ *pour = for*

Tiens, j'ai un cadeau **pour** toi.	*Here we are, I've got a present for you.*

Note: être pour quelque chose = *to be in favour of something*:

le pour et le contre	*the pros and the cons*

▼ *sans = without*

Il est parti **sans** son sac.	*He left without his bag.*

▼ *sauf = except*

Tout le monde est venu **sauf** Carole.	*Everybody came except Carole.*

▼ *selon = according to*

Selon la radio on va avoir des orages.	*According to the radio we're going to have storms.*

▼ *sous = under*

Regarde ce que j'ai trouvé **sous** le lit!	*Look what I've found under the bed!*

▼ *sur = on/upon*

Les assiettes sont **sur** la table.	*The plates are on the table.*

Note: sur is used to give fractions and statistics, or *marks out of . . .*

Un mariage **sur** trois ne dure pas.	*One marriage in three doesn't last.*
J'ai eu 13 **sur** 20.	*I got 13 out of 20.*

▼ *vers = towards*

Nous nous sommes dirigés **vers** Montpellier.	*We headed towards Montpellier.*

Note: vers translates *at about* when you are giving approximate times:

Nous allons arriver **vers** quatre heures.	*We're going to arrive at about four o'clock.*

▼ Prepositional phrases with *à* or *de*

In a number of common expressions, the pronouns **à** or **de** are used together with a noun to make a prepositional phrase. Prepositional phrases behave just like prepositions, i.e. they go before a noun and indicate position, time, etc.

Remember that when you have **à** or **de** + *the* . . . you will need to use the forms **au, à l', à la, aux** and **du, de l', de la, des** (see pages 2–4).

Here are the most common prepositional phrases:

d'après = *according to*

Elle est malade **d'après** sa mère.	*She's ill according to her mother.*

au bord de = *by the side of, by*

Tu peux t'arrêter **au bord de la** route.	*You can stop by the side of the road.*

autour de = *around*

Il y a un mur **autour du** parc.	*There's a wall around the park.*

à cause de = *because of*

Je ne peux pas venir **à cause de** la grève.	*I can't come because of the strike.*

à côté de = *beside, next to*

Elle s'est assise **à côté de** moi.	*She sat down beside me.*

au-dessous de = *below*

Qui habite **au-dessous** de ta grand-mère?	*Who lives below your grandmother?*

au-dessus de = *above*

Il y avait un grand nuage **au-dessus** de l'église.	*There was a big cloud above the church.*

en face de = *opposite*

Nous habitons **en face du** supermarché.	*We live opposite the supermarket.*

grâce à = *thanks to*

Je me suis bien amusé **grâce à** toi.   *I enjoyed myself thanks to you.*

jusqu'à = *until (time)/as far as, up to (place)*

Il reste **jusqu'à** la semaine prochaine.   *He's staying until next week.*
Ce chemin va **jusqu'à** la ferme.   *This path goes as far as/up to the farm.*

au lieu de = *instead of*

Elle a choisi du fromage **au lieu d'**un dessert.   *She chose cheese instead of a dessert.*

à partir de = *from/as from*

A partir du 15 août le magasin sera fermé.   *From the 15th August the shop will be closed.*

près de = *near*

L'hôtel est **près de** la plage?   *Is the hotel near the beach?*

quant à = *as for*

Quant à mes frères, ils arriveront plus tard.   *As for my brothers, they'll arrive later.*

au sujet de = *about/on the subject of*

Je lisais un livre **au sujet de** l'écologie.   *I was reading a book about ecology.*

VERBS
saying what is happening

▼ Groups of verbs

In French, verbs have different endings according to:

- who the subject is:

il jou**e** = *he plays*   **nous** jou**ons** = *we play*

- what tense you are using.

tu jou**ais**   *you were playing* (imperfect tense)
tu jou**eras**   *you will play* (future tense)

If you look up a verb in a dictionary or grammar book, you will
usually find the infinitive, e.g. **jouer** *to play*. From the infinitive
you can tell what group (or conjugation) the verb belongs to. This
is important because different groups have slightly different rules
for the endings in some tenses. There are three groups of regular
verbs in French:

- **-er** verbs (by far the largest group)

e.g. arriver   *to arrive*   donner   *to give*

    (A few verbs in **-er** are irregular though. Look up **aller** *to go* and
    envoyer *to send* in the list of irregular verbs on pages 151–56.)

- **-ir** verbs

e.g. choisir   *to choose*   finir   *to finish*

    (The following verbs in **-ir** are irregular though. Look up
    courir *to run,* **dormir** *to sleep,* **mourir** *to die,* **sortir** *to go out,*
    partir *to leave,* **tenir** *to hold,* **venir** *to come* in the list of irregular
    verbs.)

- **-dre** verbs

e.g. rendre   *to give back*   vendre   *to sell*

(For verbs in -**aindre** and -**eindre** see page 151. Also, see page 154 for **prendre** *to take*, and related verbs, e.g. **apprendre** *to learn*, **comprendre** *to understand*, **surprendre** *to surprise*).

Other verbs that end in -**re** and all verbs in -**oir** are irregular: e.g. **dire** *to say*, **vouloir** *to want*. For all the common irregular verbs, see the list on pages 151–56.

▼ *Reflexive and non-reflexive verbs*

You also need to notice whether or not a verb is reflexive. If a verb is reflexive, it will have the pronoun **se** in front of the infinitive e.g. **se** laver, **se** réveiller. Often reflexive verbs have the sense of an action you do to yourself: **se laver** *to wash oneself*. But quite a number of verbs are reflexive in French although we do not use 'oneself, yourself' in English: **se réveiller** *to wake up*.

You must use the right reflexive pronoun to agree with the subject of the verb. With the subject **je** you always use the reflexive pronoun **me**, with the subject **tu** you always use the reflexive pronoun **te**, etc. Here is the present tense of **se laver**:

je me lave	nous nous lavons
tu te laves	vous vous lavez
il/elle/on se lave	ils/elles se lavent

All verbs which do not have **se** before the infinitive are *not* reflexive and so do not have reflexive pronouns.

▼ Making the verb agree with its subject

In every tense in French, the verb must agree with its subject, which can be a noun or a pronoun. When you learn a tense of a verb, you will learn six forms. Here is an example with the present tense of **être**:

je suis = *I am*	nous sommes = *we are*
tu es = *you are*	vous êtes = *you (plural or polite) are*
il/elle est = *he/she/it is*	ils/elles sont = *they are*

■ **Noun + . . . et moi/+ . . . et toi**
• When the subject is *any noun or pronoun* . . . **et moi**, you
need to follow it by the pronoun **nous** and use the **nous** form
of the verb:

Ma soeur et moi, nous sommes   *My sister and I went to the café.*
allés au café.

• When the subject is *any noun or pronoun* . . . **et toi**, you
need to follow it by the pronoun **vous** and use the **vous** form
of the verb:

Lise et toi, vous avez vu le film?   *Have you and Lise seen the film?*

• When **toi et moi** are the subject, they are followed by the
pronoun **nous** and the **nous** form of the verb:

Toi et moi, nous pouvons rester ici.   *You and I can stay here.*

▼ **Activity 1**   *Making the verb agree with its subject*

Match the subjects in list (A) with the verb and the rest of the
sentence in list (B):

(A)
Ma mère et moi, nous . . .
Je . . .
Antoine . . .
Grégoire et toi, vous . . .
Tu . . .
Les deux magasins . . .

(B)
. . . sont fermés aujourd'hui.
. . . est plus grand que Chantal.
. . . ne suis pas français.
. . . es fatigué?
. . . sommes ici pour une semaine.
. . . êtes dans la même classe?

▼ *Collective subjects*
Some nouns are used in the singular to refer to a plural group of
people or things: these are collective nouns.

e.g. la police = *the police* (i.e. police officers)
le comité = *the committee* (i.e. a group)

When such a noun is the subject, in French the verb is usually in the singular:

Le comité a pris une décision.   *The committee has/have made a decision.*

However, the plural form of the verb must always be used after the following collective subjects:

la plupart = *most*

la plupart de/des (+ plural noun) = *most of (the) . . .*
un grand nombre de/des (+ plural noun) = *a large number of (the) . . .*
le plus grand nombre de/des (+ plural noun) = *the majority of (the) . . .*

La plupart des invités sont partis.   *Most guests have left.*
La plupart sont partis.   *Most have left.*

▼ Activity 2   *Verbs with a collective subject*

Choose the correct form of the verb to complete each sentence:

a   La plupart (vient/viennent) d'Espagne.
b   La police (arrive/arrivent).
c   Cette classe (travaille/travaillent) bien.
d   La plupart de mes amis (va/vont) en France.
e   Le groupe (va/vont) rester trois nuits.
f   Un grand nombre de touristes (veut/veulent) visiter ce musée.

▼ *Impersonal verbs*

Some verbs in French can *only* have the subject **il**, meaning *it*. These verbs are called impersonal verbs. For example, in both English and French the verb *to snow* (**neiger**) can only be used with the subject **il**:

Il neige.   *It's snowing.*

There are some verbs which are always impersonal in French, but can be translated by a verb with a personal subject in English. A very common example is **il faut** meaning (literally) *it is necessary.* Depending on the context, you might want to translate **il faut** by *I/you/he, etc. must/need/have to*:

Il faut aller à la banque.   *I/You/He (etc.) must go to the bank.*

Here is a list of the most common impersonal verbs in French:

- For the weather, various phrases use **faire**:

Il fait beau/mauvais	*It's fine/bad weather*
Il fait chaud/froid	*It's hot/cold*
Il fait du vent	*It's windy*
(*also* Il y a du vent)	
Il fait du brouillard	*It's foggy*
(*also* Il y a du brouillard)	
Il fait jour	*It's day/light*
Il fait nuit	*It's night/dark*

Note also:

Pleuvoir to rain: Il pleut.	*It's raining.*
Neiger to snow: Il neige.	*It's snowing.*

- Other impersonal expressions:

Y avoir

Il y a = *there is/there are*
Note: **il y a** is always singular, even when it is followed by a plural noun:

Il y a une maison.	*There is a house.*
Il y a des maisons.	*There are some houses.*

Falloir

Il faut (+ *infinitive*) = . . . *must*

Il faut payer.	*I/You/He (etc.) must pay.*

Il faut que (+ *subjunctive*) = . . . *must*

Il faut que je t'explique.	*I must explain to you.*

(For this use of the subjunctive, see page 113.)

S'agir de

Il s'agit de = *it's a question of/. . . is about*

Note: to translate (*something*) *is about* . . . you have to use the structure **Dans** . . . il s'agit de . . .:

Dans ce film **il s'agit** de Picasso.	*This film is about Picasso.*

Valoir mieux

Il vaut mieux (+ *infinitive*) = *It's better to . . .*

Il vaut mieux lui parler.   *It's better to speak to him.*

Il vaut mieux que + subjunctive = *It's better if . . .*

Il vaut mieux que tu reviennes demain.   *It's better if you come back tomorrow.*

(For this use of the subjunctive, see page 113.)

▼ Simple and compound tenses

When you are learning how to form the different tenses in French, it is useful to divide them into simple and compound tenses.

In simple tenses the verb is just one word:

e.g. j'**allais** = *I was going*   il **voit** = *he sees*

The simple tenses in French are: present, future, conditional, imperfect, past historic.

In compound tenses, the verb has two parts: the part of **avoir/être** (the auxiliary verb) and the past participle:

e.g. je **suis allé** = *I went*   il **aura vu** = *he will have seen*

The compound tenses in French are: perfect, pluperfect (and past anterior), future perfect, conditional perfect.

▼ The present tense

▼ *Forming the present tense*

To make the present tense of regular verbs, take the infinitive, drop the infinitive ending (-**er**/-**ir**/-**re**) and add these endings for each person:

	-er verbs	**-ir verbs**	**-dre verbs**
je	-e	-is	-s
tu	-es	-is	-s
il/elle	-e	-it	-
nous	-ons	-issons	-ons
vous	-ez	-issez	-ez
ils/elles	-ent	-issent	-ent
je	donne	finis	vends
tu	donnes	finis	vends
il/elle	donne	finit	vend

nous	donn**ons**	fin**issons**	vend**ons**
vous	donn**ez**	fin**issez**	vend**ez**
ils/elles	donn**ent**	fin**issent**	vend**ent**

For the present tense of irregular verbs, see the tables on pages 151–56.

▼ Using the present tense

In English we can say: *I work/I am working/I'm not working/I do work/don't work.* All these are translated by the present tense in French:

Je travaille tous les matins.	*I work every morning.*
Ne parle pas. Je travaille.	*Don't talk. I'm working.*
Je ne travaille pas le weekend.	*I don't work at weekends.*

▼ Activity 3   *The present tense*

Put the verbs in brackets in the present tense. Make sure each verb agrees with its subject:

Chère Gabrielle,

   Tu me (demander) ce que nous (aimer) faire en été. Et bien, moi j'(adorer) aller à la piscine – je (nager) tous les jours. Mes frères (jouer) au football dans le jardin, ou bien ils (promener) le chien. Et toi et ta soeur, vous (rester) chez vous, ou vous (descendre) en ville?

   Si ma copine Monique m'(inviter) chez elle, nous (écouter) de la musique. Si je (vendre) ma flûte, je (penser) m'acheter une guitare. Est-ce que tu (jouer) toujours du piano?

   Le soir ma mère (finir) son travail vers cinq heures et souvent nous la (retrouver) en ville. Si mon père est là, nous (aller) au café et nous (choisir) tous des glaces.

   Je te (laisser) maintenant, mais nous (attendre) ta carte postale de Nice – bonnes vacances.

   Je t'(embrasser),
   Laurence

■ **Etre en train de . . . = to be doing**

If you want to stress *I am (in the middle of) doing something*, you can use the expression **être en train de** + *infinitive*:

Je ne peux pas répondre au téléphone. **Je suis en train de me laver** les cheveux.

I can't answer the phone. I'm (in the middle of) washing my hair.

▼ *Special uses of the present tense*

• With **depuis/ça fait**

With **depuis** (*since/for*) and **ça fait** (**+** *time*) **que . . .** (*for*), use the present tense in French for an action which started in the past but is still going on. (In English we use *have/has been . . . ing for . . ./since . . .*)

J'attends le bus **depuis** une demi-heure.

I've been waiting for the bus for half an hour.

Ça fait deux mois **qu'elle travaille** à Codec.

She's been working at Codec for two months.

However, if the verb is negative in these sentences, use the perfect tense in French (as in English):

Je ne l'ai pas vu **depuis** un an./Ça **fait** un an que je ne l'ai pas vu.

I haven't seen him for a year.

• With **il y a**

The expression **il y a** (present tense) is used to mean *ago* when you are talking about hours, days, weeks, etc. ago related to the present.

Il y a une semaine je suis allée à Paris.

A week ago I went to Paris.

(For the use of **il y avait**, imperfect tense, for *ago*, see page 95.)

▼ The future tense

▼ *Forming the future tense*
To make the future tense of regular verbs, take the infinitive,
dropping the final -**e** in the case of -**re** verbs, and add these
endings for each person:

je	-ai
tu	-as
il/elle	-a
nous	-ons
vous	-ez
ils/elles	-ont

je	donnerai	finirai	vendrai
tu	donneras	finiras	vendras
il/elle	donnera	finira	vendra
nous	donnerons	finirons	vendrons
vous	donnerez	finirez	vendrez
ils/elles	donneront	finiront	vendront

(For the future tense of irregular verbs, see the tables on
pages 151–56.)

▼ *Using the future tense*
In English we can say *I'll work/I'll be working/I shan't work/
I won't work*. All these are translated by the future tense in French:

Il ne **travaillera** pas dimanche. *He won't work on Sunday./He won't be working on Sunday.*

■ Talking about the future
In informal French, especially in speech, people often use the
form **aller** + *infinitive* = *to be going to do something* to talk about
the future:

Nous allons rester chez mes cousins. *We're going to be staying/we'll stay with my cousins.*

If you have problems remembering the forms of the future
tense, especially for irregular verbs, you can often use **aller** +
infinitive instead.

▼ Special uses of the future tense

- The future after **quand**, **dès que**, etc.
  When the main verb of a sentence is in the future tense,
  if you also have a clause beginning with a time word like
  quand (*when*) or **dès que** (*as soon as*), you must use the future
  tense (or sometimes the future perfect) in this clause as well:

Nous vous **enverrons** la brochure
dès que nous aurons votre
nouvelle adresse.

*We'll send you the brochure as
soon as we have your new address.*

▼ Activity 4   *The future tense*

**Put the verbs in brackets in the future tense. Those marked * are
irregular – check the form of the future tense on page 151–56.**

Cher Andrew,

   Quand vous (arriver) à l'Hôtel Bonnard nous vous (donner) une
chambre au cinquième étage. Vous (commencer) à travailler dans la
cuisine le 1ᵉʳ août et nous vous (garder) jusqu'au 3 septembre.
Chaque matin le chef (décider) ce que vous (devoir*) faire. Vous
l'(aider) surtout à préparer le petit déjeuner et le déjeuner.

   Quand ma femme (descendre) en ville, vous (répondre) au
téléphone à sa place. Nous vous (demander) aussi de travailler à la
réception le mercredi soir quand nous (avoir*) des fêtes au
restaurant. Les clients (arriver) l'après-midi en général, mais je vous
(montrer) tout ce qu'il (falloir*) faire.

   Nous espérons que vous (faire*) un bon voyage, et nous
(attendre) votre lettre pour savoir à quelle heure votre train
(arriver) à la gare d'Annecy.

   Croyez, cher Andrew, à mes sentiments cordiaux,
   Alphonse LeMaître.

▼ The conditional tense

▼ *Forming the conditional*

To make the present conditional tense of regular verbs, take the infinitive, dropping the -**e** for -**re** verbs, and add the endings below for each person. (You can see that in fact the conditional is made from the future stem **+** the last syllable of the imperfect endings.)

je	-ais
tu	-ais
il/elle	-ait
nous	-ions
vous	-iez
ils/elles	-aient

je	donne**rais**	fini**rais**	vend**rais**
tu	donne**rais**	fini**rais**	vend**rais**
il/elle	donne**rait**	fini**rait**	vend**rait**
nous	donne**rions**	fini**rions**	vend**rions**
vous	donne**riez**	fini**riez**	vend**riez**
ils/elles	donne**raient**	fini**raient**	vend**raient**

For the present conditional tense of irregular verbs, see the future tense given in the tables on pages 151–56, and add the regular endings above.

▼ *Using the conditional*

In English we can say *I'd work/I'd be working/I wouldn't work/ I wouldn't be working*. All these are translated by the present conditional tense in French:

Je ne **travaillerais** pas si j'étais très riche.	*I wouldn't work/wouldn't be working if I were very rich.*

Note: For the use of tenses after **si** (*if*), see pages 107–108.

▼ Activity 5 *The conditional*

**Put the verbs in brackets in the present conditional. Those marked *
are irregular – check the form of the future stem on pages 151–56.**

Et si . . .

– Tu veux partir en vacances avec Catherine! Mais qu'est-ce que tu
(faire*) si elle tombait malade?
– J'(appeler) le médecin et puis je (téléphoner) à sa mère.
– Et si toi tu tombais malade, Sophie?
– Bah, Catherine (appeler) le médecin et puis elle (téléphoner) chez
Papa.
– Et si on vous volait tout votre argent, qu'est-ce que vous (faire*)?
– D'abord on ne nous (voler) pas tout notre argent, grand-mère. Nous
(faire*) très attention.
– Oui, mais on ne sait jamais ce qui (pouvoir*) arriver.
– Nous (aller*) au commissariat de police et nos parents nous
(envoyer*) de l'argent . . .
– Ah non, ton père (venir*) te chercher immédiatement. Il ne te
(laisser) pas toute seule.
– Dis donc, grand-mère, qu'est-ce qui (arriver) alors si toi tu étais
malade en même temps? Papa te (laisser) toute seule pour venir me
chercher? Et si Papa perdait les clés de la voiture, il (venir*) en taxi?
Et si . . .
– Sophie, il (falloir*) parler à ton père . . .

■ Translating *should* in French

In English we can use *should* instead of *would*. When *should*
means *would* it is translated by the present conditional tense:

Si je le voyais je lui **dirais** bonjour.   *If I saw him I should/would say
hello to him.*

But sometimes *should* means *ought to*, and in this case you need
to use **devoir** in the present conditional tense (e.g. **je devrais** –
see page 152) + *infinitive*:

Tu **devrais** écrire à Carole.   *You should/ought to write to
Carole.*

▼ *Special use of the conditional*

If you read newspaper reports or listen to the news on the radio or television in French, you are likely to meet a special use of the conditional tense to talk about what is thought to be happening. Reporters use the conditional because they want to say something is probably happening, but they cannot guarantee that the story is true. You will find headlines like:

Les écoles **seraient** fermées en juin.	*Schools are thought to be closing in June./It is believed/said that schools will be closed in June.*

You will not need to use this form of the present conditional yourself, but you should be able to recognise it.

▼ The imperfect tense

▼ *Forming the imperfect*

To make the imperfect tense of regular verbs, take the **nous** form of the present tense, dropping the **-ons**, and add these endings for each person:

je	-ais
tu	-ais
il/elle	-ait
nous	-ions
vous	-iez
ils/elles	-aient

je	donn**ais**	finis**sais**	vend**ais**
tu	donn**ais**	finis**sais**	vend**ais**
il/elle	donn**ait**	finis**sait**	vend**ait**
nous	donn**ions**	finis**sions**	vend**ions**
vous	donn**iez**	finis**siez**	vend**iez**
ils/elles	donn**aient**	finis**saient**	vend**aient**

Etre is the only verb with an irregular imperfect tense:

j'étais, tu étais, il/elle était, nous étions, vous étiez, ils/elles étaient

▼ *Using the imperfect*

The imperfect tense in French has two basic meanings:

• . . . *was doing*

Je **regardais** la télévision quand tu m'as téléphoné.

I was watching the television when you phoned me.

• *. . . used to do*

Quand j'**habitais** Paris, je **prenais** le métro tous les jours.

When I lived/used to live in Paris, I took/used to take the underground every day.

For the contrast between the imperfect and the perfect (or past historic), see page 99–101.

▼ Activity 6   *The imperfect tense*

Put each of the verbs in brackets into the imperfect:

La vie à la campagne il y a 60 ans
Voici ce que ma grand-mère m'a dit sur la vie à la campagne il y a 60 ans:
«Quand j'(être) jeune, mes parents (avoir) une ferme. Nous (habiter) à la campagne dans une maison qui n'(avoir) pas d'électricité. Chaque matin mon père (se lever) à cinq heures. Il (réveiller) ma mère avant de s'occuper des vaches. Moi, je (devoir) préparer le petit-déjeuner moi-même, je (boire) du lait et je (manger) du pain et du fromage. Ma mère (donner) à manger aux poules et elle (aller) chercher les oeufs. Pendant les vacances j'(aider) ma mère. Nous (faire) la cuisine et nous (vendre) le lait et les légumes. Les voisins (venir) les acheter à la ferme. Le soir, pendant que mes parents (écouter) la radio, j'(aller) voir les animaux. J'(aimer) surtout le grand cheval noir. Je lui (parler) pendant des heures, et quand il (faire) froid je lui (donner) une couverture.»

▼ Special uses of the imperfect
• With **depuis**/**ça faisait**
  With **depuis** (*since/for*) and **ça faisait** (*+ time*) **que . . .** (*for*), use the imperfect tense in French for an action which started at an earlier point in the past and was still going on. (In English we use *had been . . . ing for . . ./since . . .*)

Elle **travaillait** à Codec **depuis** deux mois.

She'd been working at Codec for two months.

Ça faisait deux mois **qu'elle travaillait** à Codec.

However, if the verb is negative in these sentences, use the pluperfect tense in French (as in English):

Je ne l'avais pas vu **depuis** un an./**Ça** *I hadn't seen him for a year.*
faisait un an que je ne l'avais pas vu.

• **Il y avait =** *ago*
The idiom **il y avait** (imperfect tense) is used to mean *ago/previously* when you are talking about hours, days, weeks, etc. ago related to a point in the past.

Nous habitions à Paris. Il y avait un *We were living in Paris. A year*
an ma mère avait vendu notre *ago/previously my mother had*
maison à Londres. *sold our house in London.*

(For the use of **il y a**, present tense, for *ago*, see page 88.)

• **Si +** *imperfect = how about . . ./what about*
Si + *imperfect* is used to make suggestions:

Si nous invitions Marc? How about inviting Mark?/What
about if we invited Mark?

▼ The past historic tense (le passé simple)

▼ *Forming the past historic*
To make the past historic of regular verbs, take the infinitive, drop the infinitive ending (-**er**/-**ir**/-**re**) and add the endings below for each person. As the past historic is never used in spoken French nowadays (see below), you will not need the **tu** and **vous** forms.

	-er verbs	**-ir/-dre verbs**
je	-ai	-is
il/elle	-a	-it
nous	-âmes	-îmes
ils/elles	-èrent	-irent

je	donnai	finis	vendis
il/elle	donna	finit	vendit
nous	donnâmes	finîmes	vendîmes
ils/elles	donnèrent	finirent	vendirent

Many irregular verbs have their past historic in -**us** (see the tables on pages 151–56). In this case the person endings are as shown below (from **courir** = *to run*):

je cour**us**
il/elle cour**ut**
nous cour**ûmes**
ils/elles cour**urent**

▼ *Recognising the past historic tense*

Nowadays the past historic tense is found only in formal written French (e.g. novels, serious newspaper reports), or occasionally in news reports read out on the radio. It stopped being used in everyday spoken French over two hundred years ago, and has been replaced by the perfect (**passé composé**). So you are unlikely to use it yourself, but you may need to recognise it when you are reading.

The past historic tense translates as: *I worked/I didn't work*.

Ce jour-là je travaillai pendant   *That day I worked for four hours.*
quatre heures.

In spoken French (and in informal writing such as a letter) you would use the perfect tense:

Ce jour-là j'ai travaillé pendant quatre heures.

▼ Activity 7   *Spot the past historic*

Underline all the verbs in this story which are in the past historic, then translate them into English.

Alex frappa doucement à la porte. Il attendit quelques instants, mais personne ne répondit. Il entendait un bruit qui venait du jardin, alors il appela Sylvie. Les deux chiens aboyèrent très fort, puis Sylvie demanda qui c'était. Elle courut ouvrir la porte à Alex. Ils traversèrent la maison ensemble et s'installèrent dans le jardin, où Mariane lisait un magazine. Il faisait beau et Alex se coucha par terre. Mariane et Sylvie apportèrent de la bière et des petits gâteaux. Les chiens en mangèrent aussi.

▼ The perfect tense (le passé composé)

▼ *Forming the perfect*
The perfect tense has two parts: the present tense of **avoir** or **être** + the past participle, e.g.

j'**ai** donné	je **suis** arrivé(e)
tu **as** donné	tu **es** arrivé(e)
il/elle **a** donné	il **est** arrivé/elle **est** arrivée
nous **avons** donné	nous **sommes** arrivés/arrivées
vous **avez** donné	vous **êtes** arrivé(e)(s)
ils/elles **ont** donné	ils **sont** arrivés/elles **sont** arrivées

Question: How do I know which verbs make the perfect tense with **avoir** and which with **être**?

Answer: Most verbs make the perfect tense with **avoir**, but there are two very important groups which use **être**:

* *All* reflexive verbs use **être** to make the perfect tense:

  se laver = *to have a wash*: je me suis lavé
  se coucher = *to go to bed*: il s'est couché

* Fifteen common non-reflexive verbs, largely concerned with movement, use **être** to make the perfect tense. You might find it helpful to remember them in a list which spells 'DRAPER'S VAN MMT 13'.

  descendre = *to go down*
  retourner = *to return*
  arriver = *to arrive*
  partir = *to leave/go away*
  entrer = *to come in/enter* (*also* rentrer = *to come back*)
  rester = *to stay*
  sortir = *to go out*
  venir = *to come* (*also* revenir = *to come back*, devenir = *to become*)
  aller = *to go*
  naître = *to be born*
  monter = *to go up*
  mourir = *to die*
  tomber = *to fall*

  La bouteille **est tombée** par terre. *The bottle fell on the ground.*

Note: Occasionally **descendre**, **monter**, **rentrer** and **sortir** make the perfect tense using **avoir**. This is only when – unusually – these verbs have a *direct* object:

Il est sorti.	*He went out.*
Il a sorti son agenda.	*He got his diary out.*

(**agenda** = direct object)

Making the past participle
To make the past participle of regular verbs, take the infinitive, dropping the **-er/-ir/-re**:

- add **-é** for the past participle of **-er** verbs:

  donné, crié, etc.

- add **-i** for the past particple of **-ir** verbs:

  choisi, fini, etc.

- add **-u** for the past participle of **-re** verbs:

  vendu, rendu, etc.

For the past participles of irregular verbs, see pages 151–56.

▼ Activity 8   *The perfect*

Put the verbs in brackets into the perfect tense. The past participles of the verbs marked * are irregular – check them on page 151–56. (You do not need to make any of the past participles in this activity agree.)

Chers Maman et Papa,
Je (arriver) à Londres hier. Le frère de Peter (venir*) me chercher à l'aéroport. Nous (prendre*) le métro pour rentrer chez lui. Quand je (sortir) du métro, j'(voir*) le Tower Bridge et j'(acheter) cette carte postale. Peter (rentrer) à six heures et nous (parler) anglais un peu. Madame Whittaker (préparer) un excellent repas. Nous (manger) beaucoup de fraises. Aujourd'hui je (se promener) à Hyde Park et Peter (acheter) un dictionnaire français.
   Est-ce que vous (donner) des carottes au lapin? Et maman, est-ce que tu (laver) mon tee-shirt pour samedi? J'espère que Yann (se réveiller) pour l'école sans moi aujourd'hui.
A bientôt et grosses bises,
Jean-François

▼ *Using the perfect*

The perfect tense in French translates *I worked, I did work/I didn't work, I have worked, I have been working.* You have to decide on the best translation in English according to the context.

J'ai travaillé ce matin.	*I worked this morning.*
	I have worked this morning.
	I have been working this morning.
Il n'a pas travaillé pendant deux semaines.	*He didn't work for two weeks.*
	He hasn't worked for two weeks.
	He hasn't been working for two weeks.

For the contrast between the perfect and the imperfect tense, see below.

▼ Choosing between the perfect and the imperfect

Often you can tell from the tense we use in English whether to use the perfect or the imperfect in French. (Look again at the explanations of the meaning of these two tenses.) In general, when you have *used to do* or *was/were doing* in English, you will want the imperfect in French.

J'**habitais** à Nantes.	*I used to live in Nantes.*
Nous **attendions** le facteur.	*We were waiting for the postman.*

But sometimes we use a simple past tense in English (*I waited, he went*, etc.) when you need an imperfect in French.

The most important times when you need an imperfect in French are:

• For an action which you repeat regularly:

Chaque jour je **partais** à huit heures.	*Every day I left at 8 o'clock.*

• For an action which **was** happening when another event interrupted it:

Nous **regardions** la télévision quand mon frère est arrivé.	*We were watching television when my brother arrived.*

- For a description of a state which lasts for a period of time, e.g. the weather, how you feel, how something looks:

Il **faisait** beau, le soleil **brillait** et je **me sentais** mieux.	*It was fine, the sun shone/was shining and I felt/was feeling better.*

Question: How long does something have to last for you to use the imperfect?

Answer: It's very difficult to give an exact answer. But there is a contrast between the imperfect and the perfect. The imperfect stresses the fact that the description **lasts**, whether for minutes, hours, years, etc. The perfect stresses the fact that this is a new event or state, a change from the previous one:

Le chat **se cachait** dans l'arbre pendant des heures.	*The cat hid/was hiding in the tree for hours.*

(**se cachait** = imperfect: the cat stayed hidden)

Le chat est sorti, puis il **s'est caché** dans l'arbre pendant des heures.	*The cat went out, then hid in the tree for several hours.*

(**s'est caché** = perfect: this is the next event)

The most important times when you need a perfect tense in French are:

- When you are recording a single, completed event:

J'**ai pris** mon vélo et je **suis allé** au supermarché.	*I took my bike and went to the supermarket.*

- When you are recording a new event or state which is a change from the previous one:

Pendant une semaine j'avais mal au pied. Alors lundi j'**ai appelé** le médecin.	*For a week my foot hurt/was hurting. So on Monday I called the doctor.*

▼ *How to translate* was/were: *perfect or imperfect?*
When you translate *was/were* into French, you have to think carefully about whether to use the imperfect or the perfect. You need the imperfect if you are describing a state which lasts for some time:

Après le match Etienne **était** fatigué et voulait se coucher.	*After the match Etienne was tired and wanted to go to bed.*

You need the perfect if you are describing a change of state. The perfect tense gives the idea of *was/were suddenly*:

J'ai été étonné quand j'ai appris qu'elle était malade.	*I was surprised (i.e. suddenly surprised) when I learned that she was ill.*

▼ Activity 9   *Choosing between the perfect and the imperfect*

Put each verb in brackets in either the perfect or the imperfect.

Quand Patrick (se réveiller), il (regarder) par la fenêtre. Le jardin (être) couvert de neige mais le soleil (briller) et il n'y (avoir) plus de nuages. Il (s'habiller) très vite. Il (mettre) un grand pullover et puis il (sortir) dans le jardin. Les oiseaux qui (venir) chaque jour l'(attendre) déjà. Il leur (jeter) le pain d'hier et il leur (mettre) de l'eau dans une vieille casserole. Mais quand le premier oiseau y (boire) un chat (s'approcher). Soudain l'oiseau (avoir) peur et (partir). Patrick (regarder) sa montre. Huit heures vingt . . . Tous les jours sa fille (téléphoner) vers huit heures et demie. Alors il (renter) dans la cuisine.

▼ Making the past participle agree

The past participle is rather like an adjective in French. This means that in certain cases it has to agree with a noun or pronoun.

- If the past participle agrees with a masculine singular noun or pronoun, it doesn't change:

Quel chapeau est-ce que tu as **acheté**? *Which hat did you buy?*

- If the past participle agrees with a feminine singular noun or pronoun, add **e**:

La maison que j'ai vue. . .   *The house which I saw. . .*

(The past participle agrees with **la maison que.**)

• If the past participle agrees with a masculine plural noun or pronoun, add **s** (unless the past participle already ends in **s**, in which case do not add anything):

Les garçons sont arrivés.   *The boys have arrived.*

(The past participle agrees with **les garçons.**)

• If the past participle agrees with a feminine plural noun or pronoun, add **es**:

Les femmes sont déjà parties.   *The women have already left.*

(The past participle agrees with **les femmes.**)

▼ *Agreement of the past participle when the perfect tense is formed with* **avoir**
When you make the perfect tense with **avoir**, the past participle agrees only if there is a *preceding direct object* (PDO). This means that the direct object comes before the verb. There are three common structures in which this occurs:

• direct object pronouns before the verb (see pages 39–40 for direct object pronouns), e.g.

Les gâteaux? Je les ai mangés.   *The cakes? I've eaten them.*

(**les** = PDO)

Remember that the pronouns **lui, leur, y, en** are not *direct* object pronouns, so the past participle never agrees with them.

• *noun* + **que** + *subject* + *verb* . . .

Les roses que nous avons achetées   *The roses which we bought are*
sont rouges.   *red.*

(**les roses que** = PDO)

• **Quel/quelle/quels/quelles** + *noun* (est-ce que) + verb?

Quelles couleurs est-ce que vous   *Which colours have you chosen?*
avez choisies?

(**quelles couleurs** = PDO)

▼ Activity 10 — *Making the past participle agree with the PDO*

The past participles in these sentences are underlined. Make them agree with any preceding direct object (PDO).

a   Mes clés? Je les ai <u>mis</u> sur la table.
b   Quels enfants est-ce que tu as <u>invité</u>?
c   Des bonbons? Non, je n'en ai pas <u>acheté</u>.
d   Ma soeur? Je l'ai <u>vu</u> samedi.
e   Je leur ai <u>montré</u> la lettre.
f   Les crayons qu'il a <u>perdu</u> sont jaunes.
g   Je peux te donner ces livres. Je les ai déjà <u>lu</u>.
h   Tu connais la boulangerie? J'y ai <u>trouvé</u> ces croissants.
i   La fenêtre qu'il a <u>cassé</u> a été réparée.
j   Quels numéros est-ce que tu as <u>choisi</u>?

▼ Agreement of the past participle when the perfect tense is formed with être

- For all reflexive verbs, the past participle agrees with the preceding direct object. In fact, the reflexive pronoun is almost always the direct object:

Elle **s'**est réveillée.   *She woke up.*

  (s' = PDO)

  But occasionally there is a noun which is the direct object, and the reflexive pronoun is the indirect object. In this case, the past participle will not agree unless the noun comes before the verb.

Elle s'est acheté une chaise.   *She bought herself a chair.*

  (**une chaise**, the direct object, comes after the verb so the past participle does not agree)

- For the group of non-reflexive verbs which make the perfect tense with **être** (e.g. **aller**, **venir**, etc.), the past participle agrees with the **subject**:

Louise est rentrée très tard.   *Louise came back very late.*

▼ **Activity 11**   *Agreement of the past*
                            participle with être *verbs*

The past participles in these sentences are underlined. Make them
agree if necessary.

a   Les enfants se sont bien <u>amusé</u>.
b   Elle est <u>arrivé</u> à quatre heures.
c   Ils ne sont pas <u>sorti</u> aujourd'hui.
d   A quelle heure est-ce que tu t'es <u>réveillé</u>, Marie?
e   Pauline et Suzanne se sont <u>embrassé</u>.
f   Tes parents se sont <u>perdu</u>?
g   Pourquoi est-ce que les garçons ne sont pas <u>resté</u>?
h   Ma soeur s'est <u>coupé</u> le doigt.
i   La chatte est <u>tombé</u> dans le trou.
j   Ma petite soeur est <u>né</u> en janvier.

▼ The pluperfect tense (le plus que parfait)

▼ *Forming the pluperfect*

The pluperfect tense has two parts: the imperfect tense of **avoir** or
être + the past participle, e.g.

j'**avais** donné	j'**étais** arrivé(e)
tu **avais** donné	tu **étais** arrivé(e)
il/elle **avait** donné	il **était** arrivé/elle **était** arrivée
nous **avions** donné	nous **étions** arrivés/arrivées
vous **aviez** donné	vous **étiez** arrivé(e)(s)
ils/elles **avaient** donné	ils **étaient** arrivés/elles **étaient** arrivées

The rules for which verbs use **avoir** and which verbs use **être** to
make the pluperfect tense are the same as for the perfect tense.
(See pages 97–98.)

   The rules for agreement of the past participle are the same as
for the perfect tense. (See pages 101–103.)

▼ Using the pluperfect
The pluperfect tense translates *I had worked* and *I had been working*:

J'avais travaillé toute la journée. Alors, le soir je voulais sortir.	*I had worked/had been working all day long. So in the evening I wanted to go out.*

▼ Activity 12 *The pluperfect*

Put the verbs in brackets in the pluperfect tense.

Cette année le sud-ouest a eu un hiver exceptionnellement sévère. La même chose (arriver) en 1963, et cette année-là la neige (durer) jusqu'en mars. Plus de cent arbres (mourir) en 1963 et on (devoir) les abattre, mais cette année on n'en a perdu qu'une trentaine.

Un psychologue a remarqué qu'en 1963 nous (refuser) de sortir souvent, et beaucoup de couples (se séparer) entre avril et mai. A Bergerac on (ouvrir) un centre d'accueil pour les couples en difficultés. Madame Loriac qui en était la directrice nous a confié qu'un jour elle (voir) dix-huit personnes. Elle a dit qu'elle (pouvoir) aider certains couples, mais pas tous. Nous n'avons pas encore vu les statistiques des séparations pour cette année.

▼ The future perfect tense

▼ Forming the future perfect
The future perfect tense has two parts: the future tense of **avoir** or **être +** the past participle, e.g.

j'**aurai** donné	je **serai** arrivé(e)
tu **auras** donné	tu **seras** arrivé(e)
il/elle **aura** donné	il **sera** arrivé/elle **sera** arrivée
nous **aurons** donné	nous **serons** arrivés/arrivées
vous **aurez** donné	vous **serez** arrivé(e)(s)
ils/elles **auront** donné	ils **seront** arrivés/elles **seront** arrivées

The rules for which verbs use **avoir** and which verbs use **être** to make the future perfect tense are the same as for the perfect tense. (See pages 97–98.)

The rules for agreement of the past participle are the same as for the perfect tense. (See pages 101–103.)

▼ *Using the future perfect*

The future perfect tense translates *I'll have worked, I'll have been working/I shan't have worked/I won't have worked*:

J'aurai travaillé huit heures aujourd'hui mais je n'**aurai** pas **travaillé** assez pour pour me payer des vacances.	*I'll have worked/I'll have been working for eight hours today but I won't have worked enough to pay for my holiday.*

▼ The conditional perfect tense

▼ *Forming the conditional perfect*

The conditional perfect tense has two parts: the present conditional of **avoir** or **être** + *past participle*, e.g.

j'**aurais** donné	je **serais** arrivé(e)
tu **aurais** donné	tu **serais** arrivé(e)
il/elle **aurait** donné	il **serait** arrivé/elle **serait** arrivée
nous **aurions** donné	nous **serions** arrivés/arrivées
vous **auriez** donné	vous **seriez** arrivé(e)(s)
ils/elles **auraient** donné	ils **seraient** arrivés/elles **seraient** arrivées

The rules for which verbs use **avoir** and which verbs use **être** to make the conditional perfect tense are the same as for the perfect tense. (See pages 97–98.)

The rules for agreement of the past participle are the same as for the perfect tense. (See pages 101–103.)

▼ *Using the conditional perfect tense*

The conditional perfect tense translates *I'd have worked/I'd have been working/I wouldn't have worked/I wouldn't have been working*:

J'aurais travaillé dans le magasin si mon père l'avait voulu.	*I'd have worked/I'd have been working in the shop if my father had wanted me to.*

For the use of tenses after **si** (*if*), see pages 107–108.

■ **Translating *should have* in French**
In English we can use *should have done* instead of *would have done*. When *should have done* means *would have done*, it is translated by the conditional perfect tense:

Si la voiture était tombée en
panne, **j'aurais appelé** le garage.

*If the car had broken down, I
should have/would have called
the garage.*

But sometimes *should have done* means *ought to have done*, and in this case you need to use the structure **j'aurais dû +** *infinitive*:

Vous auriez dû venir me voir.

*You should have/ought to have
come to see me.*

▼ *Special use of the conditional perfect tense*
If you read newspaper reports or listen to the news on the radio or television in French, you are likely to come across a special use of the conditional perfect tense to talk about what is thought to have happened (compare also the similar special use of the present conditional, see page 93.) Reporters use the conditional because they want to say something has *probably* happened, but they cannot guarantee that the story is true. You will find headlines like:

Un fermier **aurait découvert** le
trésor.

*A farmer is thought to have
discovered the treasure./A farmer is
reported to have discovered the
treasure.*

Le Président **serait mort**.

*The President is thought to have
died./Reports have come in that the
President has died.*

You will not need to use this form of the conditional yourself, but you should be able to recognise it.

▼ Using the right tenses after *si* (= if)

You need to remember which tense to use immediately after **si** and which to use in the rest of the sentence.

▼ *When* si *means 'whether'*

The first important rule is that you cannot use the present conditional/conditional perfect after **si** except when **si** means *whether* (i.e. introduces reported speech):

Il m'a demandé **si je l'aiderais.** He asked if/whether I'd help him.

(**si** = *if/whether*, so you can use the conditional)

but

Si je l'aide il me donnera If I help him he'll give me
1000 francs. 1000 francs.

(**Si** does *not* mean *whether*, so the verb immediately following it cannot be in the conditional.)

▼ *When* si *means 'if'*

In all the sentences where **si** only means *if* you must follow one of these three patterns:

- **Si** + *present tense . . . present/future tense*

Si j'**ai** un problème je **téléphone** If I have a problem I phone a
à un ami. friend.
Si tu lui **écris**, elle **sera** contente. If you write to her, she'll be
pleased.

- **Si** + *imperfect tense . . . present conditional tense*

Si tu lui **écrivais** elle **serait** contente. If you wrote to her, she would be
pleased.

Note that in English we say *if* + simple past but in French you must use **si** + *imperfect* here.

- **Si** + *pluperfect tense . . . conditional perfect tense*

Si j'**avais eu** un problème, j'**aurais** If I'd had a problem, I'd have
téléphoné à un ami. phoned a friend.

▼ Activity 13   *Using the right tense after* si

Match each part of a sentence in A with the right one in B. Look carefully at the tenses to help you choose.

A
Si nous avons le temps . . .
Si Eric avait mangé les
pommes vertes . . .
Si vous gagniez mille francs . . .
S'il pleut . . .
Si elle m'expliquait le problème . . .
Si tu t'étais cassé la jambe . . .

B
. . . tu n'aurais pas pu faire de ski.
. . . qu'est-ce que vous achèteriez?
. . . je pourrais l'aider.
. . . nous prendrons un café.
. . . il aurait été malade.
. . . tu peux prendre mon
parapluie.

▼ The subjunctive

All the tenses you have come across so far in this chapter are in the *indicative mood*. The subjunctive is another mood, or set of tenses, that is used in French after certain structures. You are familiar with the indicative to talk about what happens/doesn't happen/happened/didn't happen, etc. In general, the subjunctive is used with structures which suggest that something is uncertain or doubtful.

Il est parti.   *He's left.*

(**est parti** = perfect tense of indicative mood)

Je ne crois pas qu'il **soit parti**.   *I don't think he's left.*

(**soit parti** = perfect tense of subjunctive mood)

However, structures which use the subjunctive in French often do so because of the grammar of Latin (from which French derives). So there is not always an obvious explanation of why a certain structure needs a subjunctive. It is simplest to learn the list of the most important structures on pages 112–14.

Question: Is there a subjunctive in English?
Answer: Not like in French, where there are different subjunctive forms for all persons in four tenses (present, perfect, imperfect and pluperfect). But we can talk about a 'subjunctive equivalent' when we change a verb form or use *may/might/should* in formal English, e.g.

I would ask that you **might** consider this proposal.
He requested that she **come/should come** to see him.

Remember, though, that the French use of the subjunctive does not necessarily correspond to *may/might/should* in English, so don't assume that you need a subjunctive every time you see *may/might*.

▼ *Forming the present subjunctive*

To make the present subjunctive of regular verbs, take the **ils** form of the present indicative, dropping the **-ent** ending, and add the following endings:

je	-e
tu	-es
il/elle	-e
nous	-ions
vous	-iez
ils/elles	-ent

	-er verbs	**-ir** verbs	**-dre** verbs
je	donne	finisse	vende
tu	donnes	finisses	vendes
il/elle	donne	finisse	vende
nous	donnions	finissions	vendions
vous	donniez	finissiez	vendiez
ils/elles	donnent	finissent	vendent

Irregular verbs often have irregular present subjunctive forms. If you look them up (see pages 151–56) you will see that the **je** form usually provides the basis for **tu**, **il** and **ils**, but the **nous** form provides the basis for **vous**, e.g. present subjunctive of **vouloir** = je veuille, nous voulions.

From **je veuille**: tu veuilles, il veuille, ils veuillent

From **nous voulions**: vous vouliez

Some of the present subjunctive forms of regular verbs are the same as the present indicative forms. Go through the present subjunctive forms of **donner**, **finir** and **vendre** (above), and make a list of all the forms where the present indicative and present subjunctive are the same.

▼ *Forming the perfect subjunctive*
The perfect subjunctive has two parts: the present subjunctive of
avoir/être + *past participle*.

j'**aie** donné	je **sois** allé(e)
tu **aies** donné	tu **sois** allé(e)
il/elle **ait** donné	il **soit** allé/elle **soit** allée
nous **ayons** donné	nous **soyons** allé(e)s
vous **ayez** donné	vous **soyez** allé(e)(s)
ils/elles **aient** donné	ils **soient** allés/elles **soient** allées

The rules for which verbs take **avoir** and which take **être** are the
same as for the perfect indicative (see pages 97–98). The past
participle agrees in exactly the same way as for the perfect
indicative (see pages 101–103).

The imperfect and pluperfect subjunctives (which are based on
the form of the past historic) are hardly ever used nowadays
except in very literary writing. You won't need to use them and
will hardly ever need even to recognise them (unless you read lots
of older French novels).

▼ *Choosing between the present and the perfect subjunctive*
The present subjunctive is far more common than the perfect
subjunctive, even if other (indicative) verbs in the sentence are in
the perfect, imperfect, etc.

Il voulait que j'**aille** au concert.	*He wanted me to go to the concert.*
Elle a insisté pour que je **vienne** la voir.	*She insisted that I came/should come and see her.*

However, sometimes you need to choose between the present and
perfect subjunctive in order to make it clear whether the verb in
the subjunctive refers to the present or the past:

Je dois aller à Paris bien que je **sois** malade.	*I have to go to Paris even though I am ill.*
Je dois aller à Paris bien que j'**aie été** malade.	*I have to go to Paris even though I've been ill.*

Question: Do you have to choose between the perfect and
    imperfect subjunctive like you do between the perfect and
    imperfect indicative?

Answer: No. The choice is simply between the present and perfect tenses of the subjunctive. Nowadays, the imperfect subjunctive is not used in everyday French.

▼ *Structures which are followed by the subjunctive*
This list gives you the most common structures which are followed by the subjunctive.

• The following conjunctions (words that join parts of the sentence):

avant que . . . ne = *before*
jusqu'à ce que = *until*
bien que/quoique= *although*
à moins que . . . ne = *unless*
de peur que . . . ne/de crainte que . . . ne = *for fear that*
sans que = *without*
pour que/afin que = *in order that*
de sorte que/de façon que = *in order that/so that*
pourvu que = *provided that*

Je lui parlerai avant qu'il ne m'**écrive**.
I'll speak to him before he writes to me.

• After verbs of wishing/wanting/preferring, etc. **+ que**, e.g.

Je préfère que tu ne **viennes** pas avec lui.
I prefer you not to come with him.

But note that **espérer que** (= *to hope that*) is followed by the indicative.

• After verbs/adjectives **+ que** to express an emotion like surprise, pleasure, admiration, regret, fear, etc.

Nous regrettons qu'il ne **puisse** pas vous aider.
We are sorry that he cannot help you.

• After verbs of ordering, telling, permitting **+ que**:

Elle ne permet pas qu'on le **fasse**.
She won't let people do it.

• After all verbs of doubting, and after verbs of saying or thinking used negatively or in a question (because the negative or question imply doubt):

Je ne crois pas qu'il **soit** professeur.
I don't think he's a teacher.

- After verbs of waiting or expecting + **que**:

Tout le monde a attendu que **nous nous levions**.	*Everybody waited for us to get up.*

- After the following impersonal expressions:

il faut que = . . . *must*
il est essentiel que = *it's essential that*
il vaut mieux que = *it's better that/if*
il est normal que = *it's normal/natural that*
il est temps que = *it's time that*
il est possible/impossible que = *it's possible/impossible that*
il se peut que = *it's possible that*

> *but*

Il est probable que + indicative

il semble que = *it seems that*

> *but*

il **me** semble que/il **te** semble que, etc. + indicative

- After superlative adjectives + **que**, and after the adjectives **premier/unique/seul/dernier** + **que**:

C'est le plus beau pays que **j'aie jamais vu**.	*It's the most beautiful country I've ever seen.*

- After these indefinite expressions when you are not sure if such a thing or person exists:

un/une/des . . . qui/que = *a/some . . . that/who*
quelque chose . . . qui/que = *something . . . that*
quelqu'un . . . qui/que = *someone . . . who*

And always after these indefinite expressions:

rien qui/que = *nothing that*
personne qui/que = *nobody who*

Je ne connais **personne qui puisse** le faire.	*I don't know anyone who can do it.*

- After indefinite pronouns and adjectives like *whoever*, *whatever*, etc.

qui que = *whoever* (subject of verb)
qui que ce soit = *whoever/anyone* (object of verb)

Je ne veux pas voir **qui que ce soit.** *I don't want to see anyone/ whoever it is.*

quoi que = *whatever* (subject of verb)
quoi que ce soit = *whatever/anything* (object of verb)

Donne-moi **quoi que ce soit.** *Give me anything/whatever.*

quelque(s) **+** noun **+ que +** verb = *whatever*

Quelque problème que tu aies, *Whatever problem you have, come* viens me voir. *and see me.*

quel que soit/quelle que soit/quels que soient/quelles que soient **+** noun = *whatever . . . may be*

Quelle que soit la raison, je trouve *Whatever the reason (may be), I* que c'est bizarre. *find it odd.*

Quelque
aussi ⎫
si ⎬ **+** adjective/adverb **+ que** = *however . . .*
 ⎭

Quelque fort que tu sois, tu ne peux *However strong you may be, you* pas le faire tout seul. *can't do it on your own.*

Question: If **quoi que, quelque** and **quel que** all mean *whatever*, what's the difference between them?
Answer: You have to choose the right one depending on what follows *whatever* in the sentence.

You use **quoi que +** verb:

quoi que tu fasses = *whatever you do*

You use **quelque** (or **quelques** in the plural) **+** noun **+** verb:

quelques photos que tu prennes = *whatever photos you take*

You use **quel que/quelle que** (etc.) **+ soit/soient +** noun:

quelles que soient les couleurs = *whatever the colours may be*

▼ Activity 14   *Recognising the subjunctive*

Underline all the subjunctive forms in this conversation. Can you identify why the subjunctive is necessary in each case?

- Monique, est-ce que tu veux que je vienne te voir demain?
- Ah non, Didier, il faut que je travaille. J'ai un examen lundi et Alain a promis de m'aider.
- Oui, mais je peux venir avant que vous ne commenciez à travailler. A moins que tu ne veuilles plus me voir?
- Ecoute, Didier, j'aime beaucoup te voir mais je préfère que ce soit mardi ou mercredi.
- Et tu ne crois pas que moi je puisse t'aider?
- Mais Alain a toujours 20 sur 20 pour les math. Et c'est la seule personne qui sache m'expliquer quand je ne comprends pas.
- Et c'est le seul garçon qui ait la voiture de ses parents samedi soir, non?
- Didier, je n'aime pas que tu dises des choses comme ça! Tu ne me laisses plus parler à qui que ce soit.
- Je préfère que tu passes ton samedi avec moi, c'est tout. Mais comme je suis nul en math . . .
- Bon, je travaillerai avec Alain samedi matin et si tu attends qu'on t'appelle nous irons tous manger à la crêperie.

▼ Giving commands

When you want to tell someone to do something, you can use a command form. This is called the *imperative*, e.g.

Viens ici/**Venez** ici = *Come here*

You can see that the command can be in the **tu** form (**viens**) or the **vous** form (**venez**). There is also a **nous** 'command' form which translates *Let's* . . .

Allons plus vite.   *Let's go faster.*

▼ *Forming commands*
Non-reflexive verbs
To make the command form of non-reflexive verbs, take the **tu/vous/nous** form of the present indicative, and leave out the subject pronoun:

Choisis!	*Choose* (**tu** form)
Choisissez!	*Choose* (**vous** form)
Choisissons!	*Let's choose*

but the **tu** command form of -**er** verbs ends in -**e** (not -**es**):

Regarde! = *Look!*

The only verbs which have irregular command forms are **aller, avoir, être, savoir, vouloir**. See the list of irregular verbs on pages 151–56.

To say 'Don't do . . .', use **ne** before the command form and **pas** after it.

Ne bougez pas!	*Don't move!*

Reflexive verbs

You make the command form of reflexive verbs in exactly the same way as the command form of non-reflexive verbs. But you must put the reflexive object pronoun (-**toi**, -**vous**, -**nous**) after the verb, joined to it by a hyphen:

Lève-toi!	*Get up/Stand up* (**tu** form)
Levez-vous!	*Get up/Stand up* (**vous** form)
Levons-nous!	*Let's get up/Let's stand up*

To say 'Don't do . . .' with reflexive verbs, you change the word order to **ne + te/vous/nous + command form + pas**:

Ne t'inquiète pas!	*Don't worry* (**tu** form)
Ne vous inquiétez pas!	*Don't worry* (**vous** form)
Ne nous inquiétons pas!	*Let's not worry*

For the position of other object pronouns (**le, la, les, lui, leur**, etc.) with command forms, see page 46.

▼ Activity 15   *Commands*

First, give the command form for the verbs in brackets. Then rewrite each command in the negative, using *ne . . . pas.*

Example:
(venir) ici: Viens ici./Ne viens pas ici.

Use the *tu* command form for:

a (prendre) la bouteille d'eau minérale!
b Il est huit heures, (se réveiller)!
c (attendre), je ne suis pas prêt!
d (écouter) ce que je lui dis!
e (se dépêcher), on arrive!

Use the *vous* command form for:

f (répondre) tout de suite!
g (se reposer) maintenant!
h (finir) le petit-déjeuner!
i (mettre) les manteaux ici!
j (s'arrêter) là!

■ Other ways of giving orders or instructions

In general printed instructions (e.g. recipes, instruction leaflets and manuals), the infinitive is often used instead of the command form:

Verser le lait dans une casserole et **ajouter** le sucre.	*Pour the milk in a saucepan and add the sugar.*

If you are giving instructions to a person you know, the command form can sound rather abrupt. To be more polite, you can use the present indicative (with the subject pronoun):

Si tu arrives avant moi, **tu ouvres** la porte et **tu entres**.	*If you arrive before me, open the door and go in.*
Si vous avez besoin de quelque chose, **vous me téléphonez**.	*If you need something, phone me.*

▼ Participles

In French, as in English, each verb has two participles:

- the present participle, e.g. donnant = *giving*
- the past participle, e.g. donné = *given*

▼ *The present participle*

To make the present participle, take the **nous** form of the present indicative, drop the **-ons** ending and replace it with **-ant**:

	-er verbs	**-ir verbs**	**-dre verbs**
present indicative	nous regardons	nous finissons	nous vendons
present participle	regardant *looking*	finissant *finishing*	vendant *selling*

Most irregular verbs do form the present participle from the **nous** of the present indicative, e.g. **allant** from **nous allons.**

but there are three irregular present participles:

avoir – ayant   être – étant   savoir – sachant

Reflexive verbs keep the reflexive pronoun in front of the present participle. Remember that you always need the right pronoun to agree with the subject:

En **me promenant** par la ville j'ai vu un nouveau magasin.	*While walking through the town I saw a new shop.*

The present participle can be used in two main ways:

- As a verb, describing an action being performed. In this case the past participle does *not* agree with anything (i.e. it is invariable):

Rentrant à la maison, elle a pensé à ce qu'il avait dit.	*Going back home, she thought about what he had said.*

For the use of en + present participle (*while doing/by doing*), see page 70.

- As an adjective describing a noun or pronoun. In this case the present participle agrees with the noun or pronoun it describes:

Ces livres sont intéressants.	*These books are interesting.*

■ When you *cannot* use the present participle in French

There are two important ways in which we use *-ing* in English which cannot be translated by the present participle in French:

- In English we use *doing, going,* etc. after the verb *to be* to make continuous verb tenses: e.g. *I am staying here, They were reading.*
  These forms can *never* be translated into French by **être +** present participle. Instead, you need to use the right tense of the verb:

I am staying here.	PRESENT	Je reste ici.
We shall be leaving	FUTURE	Nous partirons.
He would be waking up.	PRESENT CONDITIONAL	Il se réveillerait.
They were reading.	IMPERFECT	Ils lisaient.
You have been sleeping.	PERFECT	Tu as dormi.
She had been talking to her mother.	PLUPERFECT	Elle avait parlé à sa mère.
They'll have been trying to phone.	FUTURE PERFECT	Ils auront essayé de téléphoner.
I would have been going to the swimming pool.	CONDITIONAL PERFECT	Je serais allé(e) à la piscine.

- In English we use *doing, going,* etc. after prepositions. In French the only preposition after which you can use the present participle is **en** (*while doing/by doing*):

Il a écrit la lettre **en écoutant** la radio.	*He wrote the letter while listening to the radio.*
Elle s'est cassé le bras **en tombant** du mur.	*She broke her arm by falling off the wall.*

All other prepositions in French are followed by the infinitive (see pages 60–70):

Il m'a donné de l'argent **avant de partir**.	*He gave me some money before leaving.*

▼ *The past participle*

The main use of the past participle is in making the compound tenses: the perfect, pluperfect, future perfect, conditional perfect. See pages 97–98 for how to make the past participle and its use in these tenses. The rules for agreement of the past participle in these tenses are explained on pages 101–103.

The past participle can also often be used as an adjective. In this case it always agrees with the noun or pronoun it describes:

Nous avons trouvé deux chats abandonnés.	*We found two abandoned cats.*

▼ The passive

Most verbs can be used either in the active or the passive. In the active, the subject of the verb does the action:

Jean	a sauvé	le chien.	*John saved the dog.*
|	|		
SUBJECT	ACTIVE VERB		

In the passive the action is done to the subject of the verb:

Le chien	a été sauvé	par Jean.	*The dog was saved by John.*
|	|		
SUBJECT	PASSIVE VERB		

The passive is made using **être** + *past participle*. In the passive the past participle always agrees with the subject of the verb.

You can use the passive in all tenses, and in both the indicative and subjunctive moods. In most cases the tense of **être** will be the same as the tense of the verb *to be* in English:

Je **suis** choqué(e).	*I am shocked.*	PRESENT
Tu **seras** blessé(e).	*You will be hurt.*	FUTURE
Il **serait** accompagné.	*He would be accompanied.*	PRESENT CONDITIONAL
Elle **était** choisie.	*She was chosen.*	IMPERFECT
Nous **avons été** vu.	*We have been/were seen*	PERFECT
Vous **aviez été** arrête(e)(s).	*You had been arrested.*	PLUPERFECT

| Ils **auront été** trouvés. | *They **will have been** found.* | FUTURE PERFECT |
| Elles **auraient été** vendues. | *They **would have been** sold.* | CONDITIONAL PERFECT |

When we use *was/were* . . . *ed* in English, though, you need to think carefully about whether to use the perfect or the imperfect in French. English uses *was/were* . . . *ed* for events (which require the perfect in French), and for descriptions of states (which require the imperfect in French):

| Paul **a été envoyé** en Italie. | *Paul was/has been sent to Italy.* | (Event, so perfect) |
| La porte **était fermée**. | *The door was shut.* | (Description, so imperfect) |

See pages 99–100 for more detailed rules about choosing between the perfect and imperfect.

▼ Activity 16 *The passive*

Rewrite each sentence in the passive.

Example:
On a sauvé Alexandre.   *Alexandre a été sauvé.*

a On distribuera les prix.
b On avait réparé la voiture.
c On prendra les billets.
d On paie le voyage.
e On a ouvert le garage.
f On perdrait l'argent.
g On a illuminé la ville.
h On aura trouvé les valises.

▼ *Verbs which cannot be used in the passive*

There is an important group of verbs which cannot be used in the passive in French: verbs which take an indirect (not a direct) object. You can recognise these verbs because the preposition à is used in front of the noun that is the indirect object.

| Je parlais **à ma soeur**. | *I was talking to my sister.* |
| Il a répondu **à ma question**. | *He answered my question.* |

Question: If you can't use a verb like **répondre** in the passive, how do you say something like *My question was answered*?
Answer: There are various ways of expressing the same idea in French.

- You can use the subject **on** and an active verb:

On a répondu à ma question.   *My question was answered./*
                                         Someone answered my question.

- With some verbs, you can use the reflexive form because it has a meaning similar to the passive, e.g. **se traduire** = *to be translated*:

Comment (est-ce que) ça se   *How's that translated into English?*
traduit en anglais?

NEGATIVES, QUESTIONS AND EXCLAMATIONS

▼ Using negatives

▼ *Not + noun/pronoun/adjective/adverb*

To translate *not + noun/pronoun/adjective/adverb*, use **pas** in front of the word:

Qui aimerait un fromage frais?	*Who'd like a fromage frais?*
Pas moi, merci.	*Not me, thank you.*
Vous aimez cette région?	*Do you like this region?*
Pas beaucoup.	*Not much.*

▼ *Not + verb*

To translate *not* with a verb, you need two words in French: **ne . . . pas**. **Ne** goes before the verb and **pas** goes after it:

Il **ne** vient **pas** ce soir.	*He's not coming this evening.*

If you have object pronouns before the verb, **ne** goes before all the object pronouns and **pas** still goes after the verb:

Je **ne** les y mettrai **pas**.	*I won't put them there.*

If you are using the perfect, pluperfect, future perfect or conditional perfect tenses, the word order is:

ne + (any object pronouns) + part of **avoir/être** + **pas** + past participle:

Nous **ne** les avons **pas** remarqués.	*We haven't seen them.*

Remember that with these compound tenses the past participle is always the last word, *after* **pas**.

Question: But when people speak French, do they always use both **ne** and **pas**?

Answer: In everyday speech, people often miss out the **ne**, but you can never miss out the **pas**. So you'll hear things like:

Je suis pas **allé** au concert.	*I didn't go to the concert.*

But in writing you should use both **ne** and **pas**:

Je **ne** suis **pas** allé au concert.

▼ Activity 1   *Using* ne . . . pas

Make each of these sentences negative by putting *ne* and *pas* in the right place:

a   Je vous connais.
b   Il est reparti.
c   Vous travaillez?
d   Claude m'en a donné.
e   Nous les reverrons demain.
f   Elle attend Pascal.
g   Vous y êtes allé?
h   Mes parents me les ont achetés.

▼ *Other negative forms*

There are some other common negative forms which, like **ne . . . pas**, have two parts. They follow the same word order.

ne . . . jamais	*never*
ne . . . plus	*no longer, not any more*
ne . . . guère	*hardly* (only used in formal style)
ne . . . point	*not at all* (only used in formal style)

Elle **ne** m'envoie **jamais** de carte postale.	*She never sends me a postcard.*
Je **ne** jouerai **plus** au tennis.	*I won't play tennis any more.*

The word order is slightly different with several other common negative forms:

• **ne . . . rien** = *nothing*   **ne . . . personne** = *nobody/no one*
If *nothing* or *nobody* is the **subject** of the verb, the word order is:

rien + ne (+ object pronouns) + verb
personne + ne (+ object pronouns) + verb

Rien ne les intéresse.	*Nothing interests them.*
Personne n'a téléphoné.	*Nobody has phoned.*

If *nothing* or *no one* is the **object** of the verb, you use the same word order as for **ne . . . pas**:

Vous **ne** comprenez **rien**.	*You don't understand anything.*

However, with **personne**, in the perfect, pluperfect, future perfect and conditional perfect tenses, **ne** goes before any object pronouns and the verb, but **personne** comes *after* the past participle:

Tu **n'**as vu **personne**?	*Didn't you see anyone?*

In more formal style you may also come across **ne . . . aucun(e)** + *noun* = no/none. **Ne . . . aucun(e)** follows the same word order as **ne . . . personne**:

Je **n'**ai trouvé **aucune** solution.	*I found no solution.*

- **ne . . . que** = *only*
  Ne always goes in front of any object pronouns and the verb, but **que** goes in front of whichever word *only* applies to. So **que** can go in different places, depending on the meaning:

Je **n'**ai visité **que ma grand-mère** samedi dernier.	*I visited only my grandmother last Saturday.*
Je **n'**ai visité ma grand-mère **que samedi dernier**.	*I visited my grandmother only last Saturday.*

Question: If **ne . . . que** and **seulement** both mean *only*, is there any difference between them?
Answer: Not really. You could use **seulement** instead of **ne . . . que** in either of the examples above. But you must use **seulement** in short phrases that don't have a verb:

Tu peux venir? Oui, mais **seulement mardi**.	*Can you come? Yes, but only on Tuesday.*

- **ne . . . nulle part** = *nowhere*
  To use **ne . . . nulle part** with a verb, put **ne** before any object pronouns + verb and put **nulle part** after the verb (or in the perfect tense, etc., after the past participle):

Je **ne** le vois **nulle part**.	*I can't see it anywhere.*
Il **ne** les a trouvés **nulle part**.	*He hasn't found them anywhere.*

● **ne . . . ni . . . ni . . .** = *neither . . . nor*
If the things *neither . . . nor* apply to are the **subject** of the
verb, the word order is:

ni . . . ni . . . ne (+ any object pronouns) + verb

Ni Armand **ni** Catherine **n'**aiment le jazz.	*Neither Armand nor Catherine likes jazz.*

If the things *neither . . . nor* apply to are the **object** of the verb,
the word order is:

ne (+ any object pronouns) + verb + ni . . . ni . . .

Elle **ne** mange **ni** les tomates **ni** les pommes de terre.	*She doesn't eat either tomatoes or potatoes.*

▼ Activity 2 *Using other negatives*

Use one of the negatives from the box below to translate the words in
brackets at the end of the sentence. You'll need to think carefully
about where each part of the negative goes.

ne . . . jamais	ne . . . plus	ne . . . rien	ne . . . personne
ne . . . que	ne . . . nulle part	ne . . . ni . . . ni . . .	

Le Baby-Sitting

Un jour je gardais ma petite cousine Catherine. Elle est sage (never). Ce
jour-là elle a disparu! Je la voyais (nowhere). Elle était dans le salon (no
more). Elle était dans la cuisine, dans la salle de bains (neither . . . nor).
Puis j'ai cherché dans sa chambre. Même sous le lit il y avait (nobody).
Et sous la table il y avait le chat (only)! Puis j'ai eu une idée. Je suis
allée dans le jardin, et la voilà assise dans une grande flaque d'eau! «Je
fais (nothing)', m'a-t-elle dit. 'Mais je voulais laver ma poupée!»

▼ *Using negatives before an infinitive*
When you need to use *not*, *no more*, etc. before an infinitive in
French, the two parts of the negative (**ne pas**, **ne plus**, etc.) are
usually put together:

Il a refusé de **ne pas** l'inviter.	*He refused not to invite her.*
Je préfère **ne rien** dire.	*I prefer to say nothing.*

The exception to this rule is **ne . . . personne** (*no one*). You put
ne before the infinitive and **personne** after it:

Il aime être seul – il préfère **ne voir**   *He likes to be alone – he prefers*
personne.   *not to see anyone.*

▼ *The 'expletive* ne*'*
In several types of sentence, in formal style at least, French uses a
ne (but no **pas**) although there is not a negative in English. This is
called the 'expletive **ne**'. Although you are unlikely to need to use
this **ne** in your own French, you'll have to recognise it to
understand sentences like the examples below.

- After these conjunctions:

avant que . . . ne = *before*
à moins que . . . ne = *unless*

> See page 112 for the use of the subjunctive after these
> conjunctions.

Il est arrivé **avant que** je **ne** sois parti.   *He arrived before I left.*

- After verbs and expressions of fearing:

avoir peur que . . . ne = *to be afraid that*
craindre que . . . ne = *to be afraid that*
de peur que . . . ne = *for fear that/in case*
de crainte que . . . ne = *for fear that/in case*

> See page 112 for the use of the subjunctive after these
> expressions.

J'ai peur que vous **ne** soyez trop   *I'm afraid you may be too tired.*
fatigués.

- After expressions of time like **ça fait . . . que/il y a . . . que/
  depuis que**, referring to the time when something last
  happened:

Ça fait deux mois que je **ne** suis allé   *I haven't been to Paris for two*
à Paris.   *months.*

- After **que** in a comparison if the second half implies a negative
  idea:

Je parle français mieux que je **ne**   *I speak French better than I write*
l'écris.   *it. (= I don't write it so well.)*

▼ Asking questions

▼ *Questions which expect the answer 'yes' or 'no'*
There are three ways in French to make an ordinary statement into a question which expects the answer *yes* or *no*:

- You can simply raise the tone of your voice at the end, without changing any of the words. Try saying:

Elle est prête. (factual voice, statement) *She's ready.*

Elle est prête? (question, raising tone of voice on 'prête')

  This is the most common way of asking questions in everyday speech.

  You can also add **n'est-ce pas?** to the end of a sentence to make a question, like we add *isn't she?*, *don't they?*, *haven't you?*, etc. in English. **N'est-ce pas** never changes, and can be added to the end of all *yes/no* questions:

Elle sera en retard, **n'est-ce pas?**   *She'll be late, won't she?*
Ils pourraient partir, **n'est-ce pas?**   *They could leave, couldn't they?*

- You can put **est-ce que** at the start of a statement to turn it into a question without changing any other words:

Est-ce qu'elle est prête?

  In this case, you don't add **n'est-ce pas** at the end.

- You can use inversion. This is more common in formal written or spoken French. For inversion, you put the verb before the subject pronoun, joining them by a hyphen:

Vous pouvez acheter des timbres. (statement) *You can buy some stamps.*
(SUBJ. PRONOUN) VERB

Pouvez-vous acheter des timbres? (question) *Can you buy some stamps?*
VERB-(SUBJ. PRONOUN)

■ Inversion

- If a verb ending in a vowel is followed by the subject pronouns **il/elle/on**, you need to put -t- between the verb and the subject pronoun:

Se **réveille-t-elle** toute seule?   *Does she wake up on her own?*

- If you use inversion with a negative sentence, **ne** goes before the verb and **pas** after the subject pronoun:

Ne pouvez-vous **pas** aller à pied?   *Can you not go on foot?*

- If the subject of the verb is a noun, not a pronoun, inversion for questions is slightly more complicated. You need to use:

Noun + verb + hyphen + subject pronoun corresponding to the noun

Claire	vient ce soir. (statement)
SUBJECT	VERB

Claire	vient-	elle	ce soir?
SUBJ (NOUN)	VERB-	SUBJ. PRONOUN	

- If you want to invert a sentence like this that is in the negative, **ne** goes before the verb and **pas** after the subject pronoun:

Claire **ne** vient-elle **pas** ce soir?   *Isn't Claire coming tonight?*

- If you are using the perfect, pluperfect, future perfect or conditional perfect tenses (i.e. compound tenses), the order for inversion is:

the part of **avoir/être**
(the auxiliary) + hyphen + subject pronoun + past participle:

Elle est arrivée. (statement)
Est-elle arrivée?

- If you use inversion with these tenses for a negative sentence, **ne** goes before the part of **avoir/être** and **pas** after the subject pronoun:

N'est-elle pas arrivée?   *Hasn't she arrived?*

On the whole, it is simpler to avoid inversion when you have compound tenses, negatives, or object pronouns. You cannot go wrong if you ask the question simply by raising the tone of your voice!

Question: But how can you ask a question simply when you are writing not talking?
Answer: Obviously you can't raise your voice when you're writing. But provided you put a question mark at the end of your sentence, the person reading will understand you mean a question:

- In a letter

Tu veux venir nous voir pendant les vacances?   *Do you want to come and see us during the holidays?*

- Or you could use **est-ce que** at the start of your sentence:

Est-ce que tu veux venir nous voir pendant les vacances?

▼ *Asking questions like* When . . . ?/What . . . ?/ How . . . ?, *etc.*
There are three ways of asking questions like *when, what, how,* etc.

- In everyday spoken French, it is common simply to put the question word at the end of the statement.

Vous êtes arrivé. (statement)   *You got here.*
Vous êtes arrivé **comment**?   *How did you get here?*

- You can use the question word + est-ce que in front of the statement.

Qu'est-ce qu'elle doit acheter?   *What does she have to buy?*

- You can use the question word followed by inversion. You need to follow the same rules for inversion as those explained in the previous section. Remember that this way of asking questions can be tricky if there are negatives, compound tenses, etc., so you might prefer to use the other ways shown above.

▼ **Activity 3**   *'Yes' or 'no' questions*

Ask the questions for the interviewer carrying out the survey ('le sondage') below. The answers of the person interviewed will help you. Remember that you can always use simple question forms rather than inversion.

Example: ....
Oui, je suis étudiante.
Question: Vous êtes étudiante?/Est-ce que vous êtes étudiante?

Le Sondage

– ....?
– Oui, je passe les vacances à Trouville.
– ....?
– Non, je ne suis pas française. Je suis anglaise.
– ....?
– Oui, nous avons loué une maison ici.
– ....?
– Non, nous ne sommes pas venus en avion. Nous avons pris le bateau.
– ....?
– Oui, je suis venue avec mes parents et ma soeur.
– ....?
– Non, je n'ai pas de frères.
– ....?
– Oui, je vais tous les jours à la plage.
– ....?
– Non, je n'ai pas vu la fête du 14 juillet.
– ....?
– Oui, je veux revenir l'année prochaine!

▼ *Common questions*

Here are examples of all the common questions, asked in the simplest ways.

Who? = **qui?**

• When *who* is the **subject** of the verb, there is one simple form of the question:

Qui frappe à la porte?   *Who's knocking at the door?*

• When *who* is the **object** of the verb or comes after a preposition, there are two simple forms of the question:

Vous regardez **qui**? **Qui est-ce que** vous regardez?	*Who are you looking at?*
Vous allez au cinéma **avec qui**? **Avec qui est-ce que** vous allez au cinéma?	*Who are you going to the cinema with?*

What? = **que/quoi**?

• When *what* is the **subject** of the verb, there is one simple form of the question:

Qu'est-ce qui fait ce bruit?	*What's making that noise?*

• When *what* is the object of the verb or comes after a preposition, there are two simple forms of the question:

Vous cherchez **quoi**, Madame? **Qu'est-ce que** vous cherchez, Madame?	*What are you looking for, Madam?*
Tu as mis l'assiette **sur quoi**? **Sur quoi est-ce que** tu as mis l'assiette?	*What did you put the plate on?*

Which/what? = **quel/quelle/quels/quelles**?

Tu as choisi **quelles cartes**? **Quelles cartes est-ce que** tu as choisies?	*Which/What cards have you chosen?*

Question: If **que/quoi** and **quel** both mean *what*, is there any difference between them?
Answer: **Que/quoi** are pronouns, and so they are used when there is no noun.

Que voulez-vous?/Vous voulez **quoi**?	*What do you want?* (*what* = pronoun)

Quel is an adjective, and must describe a noun (with which it agrees). A simple test is to see if *what* can be replaced by *which* in English. If so, you need **quel** in French:

Quel parfum est-ce que tu préfères?/Tu préfères quel parfum?	*What flavour do you prefer?* (*what* = *which*, i.e. adjective)

Which one(s)? = **lequel, laquelle, lesquels, lesquelles?**

Pour les assiettes, vous avez choisi **lesquelles?**

Pour les assiettes, **lesquelles est-ce que** vous avez choisies?

For the plates, which ones have you chosen?

▼ Activity 4 — *Who? what? which? which one(s)?*

Use one of the question forms from the box to fill in each of the gaps in the dialogue:

qui	qu'est-ce qui	qu'est-ce que	quelle	laquelle

– Bonjour Monsieur Laplace. .... se passe?
– On vient de voler ma voiture!
– .... vous avez vu?
– Il y avait deux hommes et une femme qui partaient dans ma voiture!
– .... conduisait?
– La femme.
– Et .... les hommes faisaient?
– Ils criaient à la femme d'aller plus vite!
– Et .... ils ont fait ensuite?
– Ils ont pris la route à gauche.
– .... route?
– La route après les arbres.
– Oui, mais ....? Il y en a deux.
– La première.
– Très bien, Monsieur Laplace. Je vous contacterai si nous retrouvons votre voiture.
– Mais .... je dois faire maintenant? Je devais aller à la pharmacie. Ma fille est malade.
– .... pharmacie?
– La pharmacie près de la gare.
– Oui, mais ......?
– La pharmacie Guillaume.
– D'accord, je peux vous y conduire.

How? = **comment?**

Je vais vous reconnaître **comment?**   *How am I going to recognise you?*
Comment est-ce que je vais vous
reconnaître?

Why? = **pourquoi?**

Tu l'as dit **pourquoi?**   *Why did you say it?*
Pourquoi est-ce que tu l'as dit?

Where? = **où?**

Elle a mis mon parapluie **où?**   *Where did she put my umbrella?*
Où est-ce qu'elle a mis mon parapluie?

When? = **quand?/à quelle heure?** (for clock times)

Ils doivent arriver **quand?** Demain?   *When are they due to arrive?*
Quand est-ce qu'ils doivent arriver?   *Tomorrow?*
Demain?

Ils doivent arriver **à quelle heure?**   *When/What time are they due to*
Avant six heures.   *arrive? Before six o'clock.*
A quelle heure est-ce qu'ils doivent
arriver? Avant six heures.

▼ Activity 5 — *Common question forms*

Use one of the question forms in the box to fill in each of the gaps in the diagloue.

Où?   Comment?   A quelle heure est-ce que?   Pourquoi est-ce que?

A quelle heure est-ce qu'on peut se voir?
(Le téléphone sonne.)
– Allo, Géraldine? C'est Florence. .... tu veux venir ce soir? Vers six heures, ou six heures et demie?
– Ecoute, Florence, j'ai un problème. Mes parents ne sont pas encore rentrés.
– Ils sont ....?
– A Rouen, et je dois garder mon frère.
– .... ils doivent rentrer alors?
– Vers six heures, mais je suis sûre qu'ils vont être en retard.
– Ils sont partis ....?
– En voiture. Et il y a toujours des bouchons sur la route le soir.
– .... ils n'ont pas pris le train?
– Parce que ça coûte trop cher.
– Mais qu'est-ce qu'on va faire?
– J'ai une bonne idée! .... tu ne viens pas chez nous?
– D'accord! .... il y a un bus?
– Oh, vers six heures et demie. Ça t'arrange?
– C'est parfait. Alors, à ce soir. Au revoir.
– Au revoir!

▼ Using inversion when you are not asking a question

Apart from asking questions, there is one case where you must invert the verb and subject. This is after direct speech. This inversion is quite straightforward, as you can invert either the verb and the noun which is the subject (in this case there is no hyphen between them):

«Entrez!» **dit Madame Pirou.**   *'Come in!' said Mrs Pirou.*

or the verb and the subject pronoun (with a hyphen between them):

«Entrez!» **dit-elle.**   *'Come in!' she said.*

- If the verb is in the perfect, pluperfect, future perfect or conditional perfect, and the subject of the verb is a noun, the word order for inversion is:

part of **avoir/être** + past participle + noun

«Vous voulez me voir?» **a demandé Monsieur Souche.**	*'Do you want to see me?' asked Mr Souche.*

- If the verb is in the perfect, pluperfect, future perfect or conditional perfect, and the subject of the verb is a pronoun, the word order for inversion is:

part of **avoir/être** + subject pronoun + past participle

«Vous voulez nous voir?» **ont-ils demandé.**	*'Do you want to see us?' they asked.*

- Remember with inversion that if a verb ending in a vowel is followed by the subject pronouns **il/elle/on**, you need to put **-t-** between the verb and the subject pronoun:

«Je vais partir,» **a-t-elle** annoncé.	*'I'm going to leave,' she announced.*

▼ Activity 6   *Inversion after direct speech*

Rewrite each of these sentences so that you start with the direct speech and put the verb of saying, asking, etc. at the end. Remember that you will need to invert the subject and verb after the direct speech.

Example:
Elle a dit, «Bonjour».
«Bonjour», a-t-elle dit.

a   Il a demandé, «Vous avez faim?»
b   Elle répond, «Non, je ne veux pas.»
c   Les enfants ont crié, «Maman!»
d   Madame Jouvence a déclaré, «C'est impossible!»
e   Je disais, «Voici ma maison.»
f   Elle a demandé, «Vous êtes d'ici?»
g   Il a répondu, «Ça fait 20 francs.»
h   Robert a annoncé, «C'est fermé.»

Inversion of verb and subject pronoun is also frequently used after several adverbs, particularly in formal style. These adverbs are:

à peine = *scarcely*
peut-être = *perhaps*
sans doute = *probably*

Peut-être le professeur est-il malade.   *Perhaps the teacher is ill.*

However, if you find inversion difficult, you can make sure these adverbs come later in the sentence, in which case no inversion is needed:

Le professeur est peut-être malade.

In formal written style you may also find inversion

• after the relative pronouns **que/ce que/dont/ce dont**
• in the second half of a comparison (introduced by **que**).

You need to recognise the inversion to understand such sentences, but you do not need to use it yourself:

La maison **qu'a achetée mon**   *The house which my grandfather*
grand-père s'appelle 'Les Mimosas'.   *bought is called 'The Mimosas'.*

Note: You could rewrite this sentence without the inversion:

La maison **que mon grand-père a achetée** s'appelle 'Les Mimosas'.

▼ Exclamations

In French, as in English, you can turn an ordinary statement into an exclamation by changing your tone of voice. Try saying:

J'ai gagné un prix. (factual voice, statement)   *I won a prize.*
J'ai gagné un prix! (excited voice, exclamation)

▼ Qu'est-ce que . . . ! *and* Que . . . ! = *How . . . !*

To say *How . . . !* use **Qu'est-ce que** or **Que** at the start of the sentence:

Qu'est-ce qu'il fait chaud!   *How hot it is!/Isn't it hot!*
Qu'il fait chaud!

In more formal (literary) style, you may also find **comme** used to introduce an exclamation:

Comme la mer était belle!   *How beautiful the sea was!*

▼ Quel/quelle/quels/quelles . . . ! = *What (a) . . . !*

To say *What a* + (adjective) + noun' use **quel/quelle/quels/ quelles . . . !** You need to make the adjective **quel** agree with the noun which follows:

Quelle belle couleur!   *What a beautiful colour!*
Quels vieux arbres!   *What old trees!*

■ Idiomatic exclamations

Some verbs are frequently used in idiomatic exclamations. You will probably recognise:

- **Allez!** (from **aller**: for this idiom, only the form **allez**, not **va** is used, whoever you are talking to):

Go on/Come on/Right!

- **Dis donc!/Dites donc!** (from **dire**)

Hey/That's amazing! or *Hey/I say . . .* (before a suggestion or question).

- **Tiens!/Tenez!** (from **tenir**)

Here you are! (handing something to someone) or *What a surprise/Look!*

▼▼▼
NUMBERS AND DATES

▼ Numbers

0	zéro					
1	un	11	onze	21	vingt et un	31 trente et un
2	deux	12	douze	22	vingt-deux	32 trente-deux
3	trois	13	treize	23	vingt-trois	etc.
4	quatre	14	quatorze	24	vingt-quatre	
5	cinq	15	quinze	25	vingt-cinq	
6	six	16	seize	26	vingt-six	
7	sept	17	dix-sept	27	vingt-sept	
8	huit	18	dix-huit	28	vingt-huit	
9	neuf	19	dix-neuf	29	vingt-neuf	
10	dix	20	vingt	30	trente	

40	quarante	70	soixante-dix
41	quarante et un	71	soixante et onze
42	quarante-deux	72	soixante-douze
50	cinquante	73	soixante-treize
51	cinquante et un	80	quatre-vingts
52	cinquante-deux	81	quatre-vingt-un
60	soixante	82	quatre-vingt-deux
61	soixante et un	90	quatre-vingt-dix
62	soixante-deux	91	quatre-vingt-onze
		92	quatre-vingt-douze

100	cent	201	deux cent un	1,000	mille
101	cent un	300	trois cents	1,001	mille un
102	cent deux (etc.)	302	trois cent deux	2,000	deux mille
200	deux cents				

For approximate or 'round' numbers use the ending **-aine**:

une dizaine = *about 10*
une douzaine = *a dozen*
une vingtaine = *about 20*
une centaine = *about 100*

but

un millier = *about a thousand*
des milliers = *thousands*

▼ *Fractions*

un demi, une demie = 1/2   un tiers = 1/3
un quart = 1/4   trois quarts = 3/4

When **demi** goes before the noun (with a hyphen) it does *not* agree with the noun:

un demi-kilo   une demi-heure

When **demi/demie** goes after the noun, you must use the form to agree with the gender of the noun (**demi** is *never* plural):

un kilo et demi   *a kilo and a half*
une heure et demie   *an hour and a half*
deux heures et demie   *two and a half hours*

▼ Dates

The days of the week (no capital letter in French):

lundi = *Monday*   vendredi = *Friday*
mardi = *Tuesday*   samedi = *Saturday*
mercredi = *Wednesday*   dimanche = *Sunday*
jeudi = *Thursday*

The months of the year (no capital letter in French):

janvier = *January*   juillet = *July*
février = *February*   août = *August*
mars = *March*   septembre = *September*
avril = *April*   octobre = *October*
mai = *May*   novembre = *November*
juin = *June*   décembre = *December*

To write the date at the top of a letter, etc. use:

le + day of week + number + month

le mardi 17 juin   *Tuesday 17th June*
le dimanche 24 novembre   *Sunday 24th November*

Note that French does not use the equivalent of *seventeenth* or *twenty-fourth* for dates, with the exception of *the first* which is **le premier**:

le premier mars/le Ier mars	*the 1st March*
le deux mars/le 2 mars	*the 2nd March*
le trois mars/le 3 mars (etc.)	*the 3rd March* (etc.)

To say the year you can use one of two forms:

1789 = mille sept cent quatre-vingt-neuf or
         dix-sept cent quatre-ving-neuf

But for the next millenium:

l'an deux mille = *the year 2000*

▼▼▼
PLACES, NATIONALITIES AND LANGUAGES

▼ *Continents*
Note: to say *in* + continent = **en**

e.g. en Afrique, en Europe

Noun		Adjective	
l'Afrique (fem.)	*Africa*	africain	*African*
l'Amérique (fem.)	*America*	américain	*American*
l'Asie (fem.)	*Asia*	asiatique	*Asian*
l'Australie (fem.)	*Australia*	australien	*Australian*
l'Europe (fem.)	*Europe*	européen	*European*

▼ *Countries (feminine)*
This list includes most of the countries/languages you will come across frequently.

Note: to say *in* + feminine country (i.e. most ending in **e**) = **en**

e.g. en France, en Espagne

Country		Adjective of nationality/ language	
l'Algérie	*Algeria*	algérien	*Algerian*
l'Allemagne	*Germany*	allemand	*German*
l'Angleterre	*England*	anglais	*English*
l'Autriche	*Austria*	autrichien	*Austrian*
la Belgique	*Belgium*	belge	*Belgian*
la Chine	*China*	chinois	*Chinese*
l'Ecosse	*Scotland*	écossais	*Scottish*
l'Espagne	*Spain*	espagnol	*Spanish*
la Grande-Bretagne	*Great Britain*	britannique	*British*
la Grèce	*Greece*	grec (grecque)	*Greek*
la Hollande	*Holland*	hollandais	*Dutch*
l'Inde	*India*	indien	*Indian*
l'Irlande du Nord	*Northern Ireland*	irlandais	*Irish*
l'Irlande (du Sud)	*(Southern) Ireland*		
l'Italie	*Italy*	italien	*Italian*

la Nouvelle-Zélande	*New Zealand*	néo-zélandais	*New Zealander*
la Russie	*Russia*	russe	*Russian*
la Suisse	*Switzerland*	suisse	*Swiss*
la Tunisie	*Tunisia*	tunisien	*Tunisian*
la Turquie	*Turkey*	turc (turque)	*Turkish*

▼ *Countries (masculine)*
This list includes most of the countries/languages you will come across frequently.

Note: to say *in* + masculine country:

- **au** for country in singular beginning with consonant:
e.g. au Canada, au Luxembourg

- **en** for country in singular beginning with a vowel:
e.g. en Israël

- **aux** for country in plural:
e.g. aux Etats-Unis

Country		Adjective of nationality/language	
le Brésil	*Brazil*	brésilien	*Brazilian*
le Canada	*Canada*	canadien	*Canadian*
les Etats-Unis	*USA*	américain	*American*
Israël	*Israel*	israélien	*Israeli*
le Japon	*Japan*	japonais	*Japanese*
le Luxembourg	*Luxemburg*	luxembourgeois	*Luxemberger*
le Maroc	*Morocco*	marocain	*Moroccan*
le Mexique	*Mexico*	mexicain	*Mexican*
les Pays-Bas	*Netherlands*	hollandais	*Dutch*
le Pays de Galles	*Wales*	gallois	*Welsh*
le Portugal	*Portugal*	portugais	*Portuguese*
le Royaume-Uni	*United Kingdom*		

▼ *Regions of France*
Note: Only those with different names or that are spelled differently in English and French are given.

les Alpes	*the Alps*
la Bourgogne	*Burgundy*
la Bretagne	*Brittany*
la Corse	*Corsica*
la Côte d'Azur	*the Riviera*
le Midi	*the South of France*

la Normandie	*Normandy*
la Picardie	*Picardy*
les Pyrénées	*the Pyrenees*

▼ *Towns*

Only major towns that are spelled differently in English and French are given.

Athènes	*Athens*
Bruxelles	*Brussels*
Edimbourg	*Edinburgh*
Genève	*Geneva*
Londres	*London*
Lyon	*Lyons*
Marseille	*Marseilles*
Moscou	*Moscow*
Reims	*Rheims*
Venise	*Venice*

▼ *Seas and oceans*

This list includes those you will come across most frequently.

l'Atlantique	*the Atlantic*
la Manche	*the Channel*
la Méditerranée	*the Mediterranean*
la Mer du Nord	*the North Sea*
le Pacifique	*the Pacific*

▼▼▼ VERB TABLES

▼ Regular verbs

AVOIR *to have*

Imperative: aie, ayez! *have*
            ayons! *let's have*

Present participle: ayant *having*
Past participle: eu *had*

Indicative

Present	j'ai	*I have*
	tu as	
	il/elle a	
	nous avons	
	vous avez	
	ils/elles ont	
Perfect	j'ai eu	*I had/have had*
	tu as eu	
	il/elle a eu	
	nous avons eu	
	vous avez eu	
	ils/elles ont eu .	
Imperfect	j'avais	*I was having*
	tu avais	
	il/elle avait	
	nous avions	
	vous aviez	
	ils/elles avaient	
Pluperfect	j'avais eu	*I had had*
	tu avais eu	
	il/elle avait eu	
	nous avions eu	
	vous aviez eu	
	ils/elles avaient eu	
Past Historic	j'eus	*I had*
	il/elle eut	
	nous eûmes	
	ils/elles eurent	
Future	j'aurai	*I shall have*
	tu auras	
	il/elle aura	
	nous aurons	
	vous aurez	
	ils/elles auront	

Subjunctive

Present	j'aie	*I have*
	tu aies	
	il/elle ait	
	nous ayons	
	vous ayez	
	ils/elles aient	
Perfect	j'aie eu	*I had/have had*
	tu aies eu	
	il/elle ait eu	
	nous ayons eu	
	vous ayez eu	
	ils/elles aient eu	

AVOIR contd.

Present Conditional	j'aurais *I would have*
	tu aurais
	il/elle aurait
	nous aurions
	vous auriez
	ils/elles auraient

Perfect Conditional	j'aurais eu *I would have had*
	tu aurais eu
	il/elle aurait eu
	nous aurions eu
	vous auriez eu
	ils/elles auraient eu

ÊTRE *to be*

Imperative: sois, soyez! *be*   *Present participle*: étant *being*
            soyons! *let's be*   *Past participle*: eu *been*

Indicative

Present
je suis *I am*
tu es
il/elle est
nous sommes
vous êtes
ils/elles sont

Perfect
j'ai été *I was/have been*
tu as été
il/elle a été
nous avons été
vous avez été
ils/elles ont été

Imperfect
j'étais *I was being/I was*
tu étais
il/elle était
nous étions
vous étiez
ils/elles étaient

Pluperfect
j'avais été *I had been*
tu avais été
il/elle avait été
nous avions été
vous aviez été
ils/elles avaient été

Past Historic
je fus *I was*
il/elle fut
nous fûmes
ils/elles furent

Subjunctive

Present
je sois *I am*
tu sois
il/elle soit
nous soyons
vous soyez
ils/elles soient

Perfect
j'aie été *I was/have been*
tu aies été
il/elle ait été
nous ayons été
vous ayez été
ils/elles aient été

ÊTRE contd.

Future	je serai	*I shall be*
	tu seras	
	il/elle sera	
	nous serons	
	vous serez	
	ils/elles seront	
Present	je serais	*I would be*
Conditional	tu serais	
	il/elle serait	
	nous serions	
	vous seriez	
	ils/elles seraient	
Perfect	j'aurais été	*I would have been*
Conditional	tu aurais été	
	il/elle aurait été	
	nous aurions été	
	vous auriez été	
	ils/elles auraient été	

Regular -er verbs non-reflexive

PASSER *to pass*

Imperative:	passe, passez! passons!
Present participle:	passant
Past participle:	passé

Indicative

Present	je passe	*I pass*
	tu passes	
	il/elle passe	
	nous passons	
	vous passez	
	ils/elles passent	
Perfect	j'ai passé	*I passed/have passed*
	tu as passé	
	il/elle a passé	
	nous avons passé	
	vous avez passé	
	ils/elles ont passé	

Regular -er reflexive verbs

SE RÉVEILLER *to wake up*

réveille-toi, réveillez-vous!
réveillons-nous!
se réveillant
réveillé

je me réveille *I wake up*
tu te réveilles
il/elle se réveille
nous nous réveillons
vous vous réveillez
ils/elles se réveillent

je me suis réveillé(e)
  I woke up/have woken up
tu t'es réveillé(e)
il/elle s'est réveillé(e)
nous nous sommes réveillé(e)s
vous vous êtes réveillé(e)(s)
ils/elles se sont réveillé(e)s

	PASSER contd.	**SE REVEILLER** contd.
Imperfect	je passais *I was passing* tu passais il/elle passait nous passions vous passiez ils/elles passaient	je me réveillais *I was waking up* tu te réveillais il/elle se réveillait nous nous réveillions vous vous réveilliez ils/elles se réveillaient
Pluperfect	j'avais passé *I had passed* tu avais passé il/elle avait passé nous avions passé vous aviez passé ils/elles avaient passé	je m'étais réveillé(e) *I had woken up* tu t'étais réveillé(e) il/elle s'était réveillé(e) nous nous sommes réveillé(e)s vous vous êtes réveillé(e)(s) ils/elles se sont réveillé(e)s
Past Historic	je passai *I passed* il/elle passa nous passâmes ils/elles passèrent	je me réveillai *I woke up* il/elle se réveilla nous nous réveillâmes ils/elles se réveillèrent
Future	je passerai *I will pass* tu passeras il/elle passera nous passerons vous passerez ils/elles passeront	je me réveillerai *I will wake up* tu te réveilleras il/elle se réveillera nous nous réveillerons vous vous réveillerez ils/elles se réveilleront
Present Conditional	je passerais *I would pass* tu passerais il/elle passerait nous passerions vous passeriez ils/elles passeraient	je me réveillerais *I would wake up* tu te réveillerais il/elle se réveillerait nous nous réveillerions vous vous réveilleriez ils/elles se réveilleraient
Perfect Conditional	j'aurais passé *I would have passed* tu aurais passé il/elle aurait passé nous aurions passé vous auriez passé ils/elles auraient passé	je me serais réveillé(e) *I would have woken up* tu te serais réveillé(e) il/elle se serait réveillé(e) nous nous serions réveillé(e)s vous vous seriez réveillé(e)(s) ils/elles se seraient réveillé(e)s

Subjunctive

Present	je passe *I pass* tu passes il/elle passe nous passions vous passiez ils/elles passent	je me réveille *I wake up* tu te réveilles il/elle se réveille nous nous réveillions vous vous réveilliez ils/elles se réveillent
Perfect	j'aie passé *I passed/have passed*	je me sois réveillé(e) *I woke/have woken up*

Regular -ir verbs
FINIR *to finish*

Regular -dre verbs
VENDRE *to sell*

Imperative:	finis, finissez!		vends, vendez!	
	finissons!		vendons!	
Present participle:	finissant		vendant	
Past participle:	fini		vendu	

Indicative

Present	je finis *I finish*	je vends *I sell*
	tu finis	tu vends
	il/elle finit	il/elle vend
	nous finissons	nous vendons
	vous finissez	vous vendez
	ils/elles finissent	ils/elles vendent
Perfect	j'ai fini *I finished/have finished*	j'ai vendu *I sold/have sold*
	tu as fini	tu as vendu
	il/elle a fini	il/elle a vendu
	nous avons fini	nous avons vendu
	vous avez fini	vous avez vendu
	ils/elles ont fini	ils/elles ont vendu
Imperfect	je finissais *I was finishing*	je vendais *I was selling*
	tu finissais	tu vendais
	il/elle finissait	il/elle vendait
	nous finissions	nous vendions
	vous finissiez	vous vendiez
	ils/elles finissaient	ils/elles vendaient
Pluperfect	j'avais fini *I had finished*	j'avais vendu *I had sold*
	tu avais fini	tu avais vendu
	il/elle avait fini	il/elle avait vendu
	nous avions fini	nous avions vendu
	vous aviez fini	vous aviez vendu
	ils/elles avaient fini	ils/elles avaient vendu
Past Historic	je finis *I finished*	je vendis *I sold*
	il/elle finit	il/elle vendit
	nous finîmes	nous vendîmes
	ils/elles finirent	ils/elles vendirent
Future	je finirai *I will finish*	je vendrai *I will sell*
	tu finiras	tu vendras
	il/elle finira	il/elle vendra
	nous finirons	nous vendrons
	vous finirez	vous vendrez
	ils/elles finiront	ils/elles vendront
Present Conditional	je finirais *I would finish*	je vendrais *I would sell*
	tu finirais	tu vendrais
	il/elle finirait	il/elle vendrait
	nous finirions	nous vendrions
	vous finiriez	vous vendriez
	ils/elles finiraient	ils/elles vendraient

FINIR contd.		VENDRE contd.	
Perfect	j'aurais fini *I would have finished*	j'aurais vendu *I would have sold*	
Conditional	tu aurais fini	tu aurais vendu	
	il/elle aurait fini	il/elle aurait vendu	
	nous aurions fini	nous aurions vendu	
	vous auriez fini	vous auriez vendu	
	ils/elles auraient fini	ils/elles auraient vendu	

Subjunctive

Present	je finisse *I finish*	je vende *I sell*
	tu finisses	tu vendes
	il/elle finisse	il/elle vende
	nous finissions	nous vendions
	vous finissiez	vous vendiez
	ils/elles finissent	ils/elles vendent
Perfect	j'aie fini *I finished/have finished*	j'aie vendu *I sold/have sold*

There are five groups of regular **-er** verbs which need minor spelling changes in some tenses. In all other tenses, these groups are conjugated exactly like *passer*. For tenses where only the **je** form is given, see pages 86–111 for the endings for all other persons.

a) Most verbs in **-eter** and **-eler** double the **t** or the **l** in parts of the present tense and throughout the future and conditional tenses.

JETER *to throw*		APPELER *to call*	

Indicative

Present	je jette *I throw*	j'appelle *I call*
	tu jettes	tu appelles
	il/elle jette	il/elle appelle
	nous jetons	nous appelons
	vous jetez	vous appelez
	ils/elles jettent	ils/elles appellent
Future	je jetterai *I will throw*	j'appellerai *I will call*
Present Conditional	je jetterais *I would throw*	j'appellerais *I would call*

Subjunctive

Present	je jette *I throw*	j'appelle *I call*
	tu jettes	tu appelles
	il/elle jette	il/elle appelle
	nous jetions	nous appelions
	vous jetiez	vous appeliez
	ils/elles jettent	ils/elles appellent

b) Verbs in **-emer**, **-ener**, **-ever** and some verbs in **-eler** (geler – *to freeze*, modeler – *to model*, peler – *to peel*) and **-eter** (acheter – *to buy*) need a grave accent (è) in parts of the present indicative and subjunctive tenses and throughout the future and present conditional tenses.

LEVER *to raise*   **ACHETER** *to buy*

Indicative

Present
je lève   *I raise*   j'achète   *I buy*
tu lèves   tu achètes
il/elle lève   il/elle achète
nous levons   nous achetons
vous levez   vous achetez
ils/elles lèvent   ils/elles achètent

Future   je lèverai   *I will raise*   j'achèterai   *I will buy*

Present
Conditional je lèverais   *I would raise*   j'achèterais   *I would buy*

Subjunctive

Present   je lève   *I raise*   j'achète   *I buy*
          tu lèves   tu achètes
          il/elle lève   il/elle achète
          nous levions   nous achetions
          vous leviez   vous achetiez
          ils/elles lèvent   ils/elles achètent

c) Verbs in **-cer** and **-ger** need **ç** or **ge** in parts of the present indicative, imperfect and past historic, and in the present participle.

MANGER *to eat*   **LANCER** *to throw*

Indicative

Present
je mange   *I eat*   je lance   *I throw*
tu manges   tu lances
il/elle mange   il/elle lance
nous mangeons   nous lançons
vous mangez   vous lancez
ils/elles mangent   ils/elles lancent

Imperfect
je mangeais *I was eating*   je lançais   *I was throwing*
tu mangeais   tu lançais
il/elle mangeait   il/elle lançait
nous mangions   nous lancions
vous mangiez   vous lanciez
ils/elles mangeaient   ils/elles lançaient

Past
Historic
je mangeai   *I ate*   je lançai   *I threw*
il/elle mangea   il/elle lança
nous mangeâmes   nous lançâmes
ils/elles mangèrent   ils/elles lancèrent

Present
participle
mangeant   *eating*   lançant   *throwing*

d) Verbs in **-érer** need to change the accute accent (é) to a grave accent (è) in parts of the present indicative and subjunctive..

PRÉFÉRER *to prefer*

	Indicative		**Subjunctive**	
Present	je préfère	*I prefer*	je préfère	*I prefer*
	tu préfères		tu préfères	
	il/elle préfère		il/elle préfère	
	nous préférons		nous préférions	
	vous préférez		vous préfériez	
	ils/elles préfèrent		ils/elles préfèrent	

e) Verbs in **-oyer** and **-uyer** change the **y** to **i** in parts of the present indicative and subjunctive and throughout the future and present conditional tenses.

EMPLOYER *to use, employ*

	Indicative		**Subjunctive**	
Present	j'emploie	*I use*	j'emploie	*I use*
	tu emploies		tu emploies	
	il/elle emploie		il/elle emploie	
	nous employons		nous employions	
	vous employez		vous employiez	
	ils/elles emploient		ils/elles emploient	
Future	j'emploierai	*I will use*		
Present Conditional	j'emploierais	*I would use*		

Conjugation of verbs in -aindre and -eindre

These verbs differ from the regular **-dre** conjugation like vendre.

PEINDRE *to paint*

	Indicative		**Subjunctive**	
Present	je peins	*I paint*	je peigne	*I paint*
	tu peins		tu peignes	
	il/elle peint		il/elle peigne	
	nous peignons		nous peignions	
	vous peignez		vous peigniez	
	ils/elles peignent		ils/elles peignent	
Perfect	j'ai peint	*I painted/have painted*		
Past Historic	je peignis	*I painted*		
	il/elle peignit			
	nous peignîmes			
	ils/elles peignirent			
Present participle	peignant	*painting*		

Conjugation of common irregular verbs

	ALLER *to go*	**S'ASSEOIR** *to sit down*	**BOIRE** *to drink*
Present indicative	je vais *I go* tu vas il/elle va nous allons vous allez ils/elles vont	je m'assieds *I sit down* tu t'assieds il/elle s'assied nous nous asseyons vous vous asseyez ils/elles s'asseyent	je bois *I drink* tu bois il/elle boit nous buvons vous buvez ils/elles boivent

Perfect	je suis allé(e)
	   I went/have gone
		je me suis assis(e)
		   I sat down/have sat down
			j'ai bu
			   I drank/have drunk

Imperfect	j'allais
	   I was going
		je m'asseyais
		   I was sitting down
			je buvais
			   I was drinking

Past Historic	j'allai
	   I went
		je m'assis
		   I sat down
			je bus
			   I drank

Future	j'irai
	   I will go
		je m'assiérai
		   I will sit down
			je boirai
			   I will drink

Present subjunctive	j'aille *I go* tu ailles il/elle aille nous allions vous alliez ils/elles aillent	je m'asseye *I sit down* tu t'asseyes il/elle s'asseye nous nous asseyions vous vous asseyiez ils/elles s'asseyent	je boive *I drink* tu boives il/elle boive nous buvions vous buviez ils/elles boivent
Present participle	allant *going*	s'asseyant *sitting down*	buvant *drinking*
Imperative	va (*but note* vas-y), allez! allons!	assieds-toi, asseyez-vous! asseyons-nous!	bois, buvez! buvons!

	CONDUIRE *to drive*	**CONNAÎTRE** *to know*	**COURIR** *to run*
Present indicative	je conduis *I drive* tu conduis il/elle conduit nous conduisons vous conduisez ils/elles conduisent	je connais *I know* tu connais il/elle connaît nous connaissons vous connaissez ils/elles connaissent	je cours *I run* tu cours il/elle court nous courons vous courez ils/elles courent

Perfect	j'ai conduit
	   I drove/have driven
		j'ai connu
		   I knew/have known
			j'ai couru
			   I ran/have run

Imperfect	je conduisais
	   I was driving
		je connaissais
		   I used to know
			je courais
			   I was running

Past Historic	je conduisis
	   I drove
		je connus
		   I knew
			je courus
			   I ran

Future	je conduirai
	   I will drive
		je connaîtrai
		   I will know
			je courrai
			   I will run

Present subjunctive	je conduise *I drive*	je connaisse *I know*	je coure *I run*
	tu conduises	tu connaisses	tu coures
	il/elle conduise	il/elle connaisse	il/elle coure
	nous conduisions	nous connaissions	nous courions
	vous conduisiez	vous connaissiez	vous couriez
	ils/elles conduisent	ils/elles connaissent	ils/elles courent
Present participle	conduisant *driving*	connaissant *knowing*	courant *running*
Imperative	conduis, conduisez!	connais, connaissez!	cours, courez!
	conduisons!	connaissons!	courons!

	CROIRE *to think, believe*	**DEVOIR** *to have to, must*	**DIRE** *to say*
Present indicative	je crois *I think*	je dois *I have to*	je dis *I say*
	tu crois	tu dois	tu dis
	il/elle croit	il/elle doit	il/elle dit
	nous croyons	nous devons	nous disons
	vous croyez	vous devez	vous dites
	ils/elles croient	ils/elles doivent	ils/elles disent
Perfect	j'ai cru *I thought/have though*	j'ai dû *I had to/have had to*	j'ai dit *I said/have said*
Imperfect	je croyais *I was thinking*	je devais *I was having to*	je disais *I was saying*
Past Historic	je crus *I thought*	je dus *I had to*	je dis *I said*
Future	je croirai *I will think*	je devrai *I will have to*	je dirai *I will say*
Present subjunctive	je croie *I think*	je doive *I have to*	je dise *I say*
	tu croies	tu doives	tu dises
	il/elle croie	il/elle doive	il/elle dise
	nous croyions	nous devions	nous disions
	vous croyiez	vous deviez	vous disiez
	ils/elles croient	ils/elles doivent	ils/elles disent
Present participle	croyant *thinking*	devant *having to*	disant *saying*
Imperative	crois, croyez!		dis, dites!
	croyons!		disons!

	DORMIR *to sleep*	**ÉCRIRE** *to write*	**ENVOYER** *to send*
Present indicative	je dors *I sleep*	j'écris *I write*	j'envoie *I send*
	tu dors	tu écris	tu envoies
	il/elle dort	il/elle écrit	il/elle envoie
	nous dormons	nous écrivons	nous envoyons
	vous dormez	vous écrivez	vous envoyez
	ils/elles dorment	ils/elles écrivent	ils/elles envoient

Perfect	j'ai dormi *I slept/have slept*	j'ai écrit *I wrote/have written*	j'ai envoyé *I sent/have sent*
Imperfect	je dormais *I was sleeping*	j'écrivais *I was writing*	j'envoyais *I was sending*
Past Historic	je dormis *I slept*	j'écrivis *I wrote*	j'envoyai *I sent*
Future	je dormirai *I will sleep*	j'écrirai *I will write*	j'enverrai *I will send*
Present subjunctive	je dorme *I sleep* tu dormes il/elle dorme nous dormions vous dormiez ils/elles dorment	j'écrive *I write* tu écrives il/elle écrive nous écrivions vous écriviez ils/elles écrivent	j'envoie *I send* tu envoies il/elle envoie nous envoyions vous envoyiez ils/elles envoient
Present participle	dormant *sleeping*	écrivant *writing*	envoyant *sending*
Imperative	dors, dormez! dormons!	écris, écrivez! écrivons!	envoie, envoyez! envoyons!

	FAIRE *to do, make*	**FALLOIR** *to have to, must* *N.B. an impersonal verb, only used with the subject* **il** *(see p. 85)*	**LIRE** *to read*
Present indicative	je fais *I do* tu fais il/elle fait nous faisons vous faites ils/elles font	 il faut *must*	je lis *I read* tu lis il/elle lit nous lisons vous lisez ils/elles lisent
Perfect	j'ai fait *I did/have done*	il a fallu *had to/has had to*	j'ai lu *I read/have read*
Imperfect	je faisais *I was doing*	il fallait *was having to*	je lisais *I was reading*
Past Historic	je fis *I did*	il fallut *had to*	je lus *I read*
Future	je ferai *I will do*	il faudra *will have to*	je lirai *I will read*
Present subjunctive	je fasse *I do* tu fasses il/elle fasse nous fassions vous fassiez ils/elles fassent	 il faille *must*	je lise *I read* tu lises il/elle lise nous lisions vous lisiez ils/elles lisent
Present participle	faisant *doing*		lisant *reading*
Imperative	fais, faites! faisons!		lis, lisez! lisons!

	METTRE *to put*	**MOURIR** *to die*	**NAÎTRE** *to be born*
Present indicative	je mets *I put* tu mets il/elle met nous mettons vous mettez ils/elles mettent	je meurs *I die* tu meurs il/elle meurt nous mourons vous mourez ils/elles meurent	je nais *I am born* tu nais il/elle naît nous naissons vous naissez ils/elles naissent
Perfect	j'ai mis *I put/have put*	je suis mort(e) *I died/have died*	je suis né(e) *I was born*
Imperfect	je mettais *I was putting*	je mourais *I was dying*	je naissais *I was being born*
Past Historic	je mis *I put*	je mourus *I died*	je naquis *I was born*
Future	je mettrai *I will put*	je mourrai *I will die*	je naîtrai *I will be born*
Present subjunctive	je mette *I put* tu mettes il/elle mette nous mettions vous mettiez ils/elles mettent	je meure *I die* tu meures il/elle meure nous mourions vous mouriez ils/elles meurent	je naisse *I am born* tu naisses il/elle naisse nous naissions vous naissiez ils/elles naissent
Present participle	mettant *putting*	mourant *dying*	naissant *being born*
Imperative	mets, mettez! mettons!	meurs, mourez! mourons!	

	OUVRIR *to open*	**PARTIR** *to leave*	**PLAIRE** *to please*
Present indicative	j'ouvre *I open* tu ouvres il/elle ouvre nous ouvrons vous ouvrez ils/elles ouvrent	je pars *I leave* tu pars il/elle part nous partons vous partez ils/elles partent	je plais *I please* tu plais il/elle plaît nous plaisons vous plaisez ils/elles plaisent
Perfect	j'ai ouvert *I opened/have*	je suis parti(e) *I left/have left*	j'ai plu *I pleased/have pleased*
Imperfect	j'ouvrais *I was opening*	je partais *I was leaving*	je plaisais *I was pleasing*
Past Historic	j'ouvris *I opened*	je partis *I left*	je plus *I pleased*
Future	j'ouvrirai *I will open*	je partirai *I will leave*	je plairai *I will please*

Present subjunctive	j'ouvre *I open*	je parte *I leave*	je plaise *I please*
	tu ouvres	tu partes	tu plaises
	il/elle ouvre	il/elle parte	il/elle plaise
	nous ouvrions	nous partions	nous plaisions
	vous ouvriez	vous partiez	vous plaisiez
	ils/elles ouvrent	ils/elles partent	ils/elles plaisent
Present participle	ouvrant *opening*	partant *leaving*	plaisant *pleasing*
Imperative	ouvre, ouvrez!	pars, partez!	
	ouvrons!	partons!	

	PLEUVOIR *to rain*	**POUVOIR** *to be able, can*	**PRENDRE** *to take*
	N.B. an impersonal verb, only used with the subject **il** (see p. 85)		
Present indicative		je peux (puis*) *I can*	je prends *I take*
		tu peux	tu prends
	il pleut *it is raining*	il/elle peut	il/elle prend
		nous pouvons	nous prenons
		vous pouvez	vous prenez
		ils/elles peuvent	ils/elles prennent
Perfect	il a plu *it rained/has rained*	j'ai pu *I was able*	j'ai pris *I took/have taken*
Imperfect	il pleuvait *it was raining*	je pouvais *I was able*	je prenais *I was taking*
Past Historic	il plut *it rained*	je pus *I was able*	je pris *I took*
Future	il pleuvra *it will rain*	je pourrai *I will be able*	je prendrai *I will take*
Present subjunctive		je puisse *I can*	je prenne *I take*
		tu puisses	tu prennes
	il pleuve *it rains*	il/elle puisse	il/elle prenne
		nous puissions	nous prenions
		vous puissiez	vous preniez
		ils/elles puissent	ils/elles prennent
Present participle	pleuvant *raining*	pouvant *being able*	prenant *taking*
Imperative			prends, prenez!
			prenons!

*Note: puis *is commonly used in the question form* 'puis-je?'

	RECEVOIR, to receive, get	**RIRE** to laugh	**SAVOIR** to know
Present indicative	je reçois *I receive* tu reçois il/elle reçoit nous recevons vous recevez ils/elles reçoivent	je ris *I laugh* tu ris il/elle rit nous rions vous riez ils/elles rient	je sais *I know* tu sais il/elle sait nous savons vous savez ils/elles savent

Perfect	j'ai reçu
	  I received/have received
		j'ai ri
		  I laughed/have laughed
			j'ai su
			  I knew/have known

Imperfect	je recevais
	  I was receiving
		je riais
		  I was laughing
			je savais
			  I used to know

Past Historic	je reçus
	  I received
		je ris
		  I laughed
			je sus
			  I knew

Future	je recevrai
	  I will receive
		je rirai
		  I will laugh
			je saurai
			  I will know

Present subjunctive	je reçoive *I receive* *tu reçoives* il/elle reçoive nous recevions vous receviez ils/elles reçoivent	je rie *I laugh* *tu ries* il/elle rie nous riions vous riiez ils/elles rient	je sache *I know* *tu saches* il/elle sache nous sachions vous sachiez ils/elles sachent
Present participle	recevant *receiving*	riant *laughing*	sachant *knowing*
Imperative	reçois, recevez! recevons!	ris, riez! rions!	sache, sachez! sachons!

	SUIVRE to follow	**TENIR** to hold	**VENIR** to come
Present indicative	je suis *I follow* tu suis il/elle suit nous suivons vous suivez ils/elles suivent	je tiens *I hold* tu tiens il/elle tient nous tenons vous tenez ils/elles tiennent	je viens *I come* tu viens il/elle vient nous venons vous venez ils/elles viennent

Perfect	j'ai suivi
	  I followed/have followed
		j'ai tenu
		  I held/have held
			je suis venu(e)
			  I came/have come

Imperfect	je suivais
	  I was following
		je tenais
		  I was holding
			je venais
			  I was coming

Past Historic	je suivis
	  I followed
		je tins
		  I held
		il/elle tint
		nous tînmes
		ils/elles tinrent
			je vins
			  I came
			il/elle vint
			nous vînmes
			ils/elles vinrent

Future	je suivrai *I will follow*		je tiendrai *I will hold*		je viendrai *I will come*

Present subjunctive	je suive *I follow* tu suives il/elle suive nous suivions vous suiviez ils/elles suivent	je tienne *I hold* tu tiennes il/elle tienne nous tenions vous teniez ils/elles tiennent	je vienne *I come* tu viennes il/elle vienne nous venions vous veniez ils/elles viennent

Present participle	suivant *following*	tenant *holding*	venant *coming*

Imperative	suis, suivez! suivons!	tiens, tenez! tenons!	viens, venez! venons!

VOIR *to see*   **VOULOIR** *to want*

Present indicative	je vois *I see* tu vois il/elle voit nous voyons vous voyez ils/elles voient	je veux *I want* tu veux il/elle veut nous voulons vous voulez ils/elles veulent
Perfect	j'ai vu *I saw/have seen*	j'ai voulu *I wanted/have wanted*
Imperfect	je voyais *I was seeing*	je voulais *I was wanting*
Past Historic	je vis *I saw*	je voulus *I wanted*
Future	je verrai *I will see*	je voudrai *I will want*
Present subjunctive	je voie *I see* tu voies il/elle voie nous voyions vous voyiez ils/elles voient	je veuille *I want* tu veuilles il/elle veuille nous voulions vous vouliez ils/elles veuillent
Present participle	voyant *seeing*	voulant *waiting*
Imperative	vois, voyez! voyons!	veuille, veuillez! *please*

▼▼▼
ANSWERS TO ACTIVITIES

▼ Nouns and Articles

Activity 1
Le Journal, la méteo, la température, l'eau, Les gens, le soleil, le matin, l'après-midi, La semaine, le retour, la France, la pluie.

Activity 2
a au policier
b au téléphone
c aux autorités
d au cinéma

e au magasin
f à la piscine
g à l'hôpital
h aux clients.

Activity 3
Des gâteaux, du chocolat, pas de chocolat, des abricots, plus d'abricots, de la bière, de la limonade, plus de limonade, de l'eau, des glaces, plus d'argent.

Activity 4
X reporter, X détective, X secrétaire, la semaine, des enfants, des garçons, un chien, X imperméable, le visage, des voitures/les voitures, le parking.

Activity 5
Masculine: dimanche, jardin, pommier, assortiment, poulet, père, dessert, champagne.
Feminine: fête, villa, plage, salade, bouteille, cave, glace.

Activity 6
a la personne
b la Chine et le Japon
c le latin
d la tante, le grand-père
e le mardi

f La Suisse, le Luxembourg
g Le printemps
h la poire, la banane, le kiwi
i la victime
j la tomate, le concombre.

Activity 7
a Le shampooing
b la saison
c le chocolat
d la solution
e La promenade

f le village, la plage
g La solitude
h le document
i la télévision
j la sincérité, la qualité.

Activity 8
a clés
b bijoux
c trous
d dinosaures
e yeux
f héros

g jeux
h animaux
i Messieurs
j travaux
k Arnould
l Mesdames.

▼ *Adjectives*

Activity 1
sensationnel, anglais, français, incroyable, rapide, ancienne, jaloux, courageuse.

Activity 2
une grande ferme, un pullover jaune, une veste noire, la veste est grise, la fille . . . petite, une robe verte, des chaussures vertes, la ferme est jolie, fleurs rouges, la porte est ouverte, elle est fermée, un prix formidable, de gros canards très drôles, vous êtes brillante, une semaine gratuite.

Activity 3
a spéciaux
b ancienne
c active
d départementale
e traditionnelles
f internationaux
g fabuleuses
h régionaux
i sensationnelle
j mystérieuses.

Activity 4
bel appartement, températures douces, longues journées ensoleillées, lumière blanche, bonnes vacances, famille grecque . . . gentille, moto neuve, autres pays, nouvelle brochure, prix bas, vieil hôtel, plages publiques, hôtels turcs . . . pleins, touristes fous, bel endroit tranquille, maisons blanches, terre sèche, enfants impossibles.

Activity 5
a une valise bleue et des chaussures marron
b une cravate bleu marine
c une veste noire et des gants vert clair
d des chaussures rouges et des chaussettes gris foncé
e Les gâteaux sentent bon.
f Elle travaille trop dur.
g Continuez tout droit!
h Les pommes coûtent cher.

Activity 6
a ce/mon petit/vieux/nouveau train rouge
b Ce petit/nouveau/vieux/vaste jardin/ce jardin abandonné
c un nouveau/vieux programme
d toutes les sandales grecques/toutes les vieilles sandales; le petit/nouveau/vieux/troisième magasin; le petit/nouveau/vieux port.
e les vieux chiens
f toutes les vieilles maisons grecques.

Activity 7
plus grande que moi, aussi grande que ma mère, le plus petit de la famille, meilleurs que moi/plus forts que moi, plus forts que moi, pas si fort, le meilleur footballer du monde, le meilleur artiste de ma classe, aussi grand que toi.

Activity 8
a ses clés
b sa photo
c leurs vélos
d ta/votre gomme
e les cheveux
f son manteau
g notre chambre
h sa machine
i Les yeux me font mal.
j La jambe te fait mal?

Activity 9
cet arbre, ces feux, cette . . . route, ces . . . maisons, cette voiture, cet homme, ce camion, ce rond-point, cet hôtel, ces magasins, cette boulangerie, ce café.

▼ *Adverbs*

Activity 1
rapidement, silencieusement, immédiatement, miraculeusement, Naturellement, facilement, exceptionnellement, finalement, Heureusement.

Activity 2

a	énormément	f	lentement
b	gentiment	g	profondément
c	vraiment	h	bien
d	constamment	i	mal.
e	récemment		

Activity 3

a	moins de	f	Combien de
b	un peu de	g	tant de
c	Peu des	h	trop de
d	beaucoup de	i	assez d'
e	plus de	j	beaucoup de.

Activity 4
plus doucement; plus souvent que moi; mieux que vous; moins bien que mon chat; plus vous me dérangez, plus je vais chanter; Plus vous chantez, plus j'ai envie de crier; plus patiemment; plus poliment, moins agressivement; aussi vite que possible.

▼ *Pronouns*

Activity 1
Ça, Tu, j', toi, t', l', lui, il, Je, il, me, C', Tu, on, toi, on.

Activity 2

a	Elle	e	Elles
b	Ils	f	Ils
c	qu'on	g	Elles
d	qu'elles	h	On/Elle.

Activity 3

a	tu les achètes	d	Je veux la louer
b	ne l'avez pas vu	e	Nous les réserverons
c	Elle les invite	f	me la passer.

Activity 4

a	Vous lui avez déjà parlé?	d	Vous ne m'avez pas répondu.
b	Nous leur envoyons les livres.	e	Je ne te/vous parle pas!
c	Qui lui a donné cette nouvelle?	f	Je leur donnerai le cadeau.

Activity 5
les, les, le, l', le, lui, lui, les, leur.

Activity 6

a Il m'en faut
b Vous en voulez
c Tu y es allé
d Je n'en ai pas
e Vous y restez

f J'en suis partie
g y joue
h s'y intéressent
i Elle en est
j Tu t'en souviens.

Activity 7

a Elle les y a vus.
b Nous ne leur en parlerons pas.
c Pourquoi est-ce que vous nous les envoyez?
d Tu peux me la montrer?
e Martine vous en a acheté?

f Mes parents ne nous y trouveront pas.
g Offrez-leur-en!
h Explique-le-nous!
i Allez-y!
j Cachez-les-moi!

Activity 8

a elle
b eux
c lui, moi
d nous

e toi/vous, elle
f vous
g elles, lui
h eux.

Activity 9

a les tiens
b la vôtre
c la leur, la nôtre
d la sienne
e le sien

f les nôtres
g les leurs
h le sien
i les miennes.

Activity 10
celui-là, ceux-ci, celles-ci, celui-là, celles-là, celui-ci, celle-ci, celle-là, celui-ci, celui-là, celui-ci.

Activity 11
quelque chose, rien, quelqu'un, On/Quelqu'un, rien, rien/pas grand-chose, personne, on/quelqu'un, qu'on/que quelqu'un, personne.

Activity 12

a ce que
b où
c que
d ce qui

e qui
f où
g que
h ce que.

▼ *Prepositions*

Activity 1
a un camion arriver
b un enfant pleurer
c son fils parler
d les garçons sauter du mur
e Gisèle nager
f jouer de la guitare
g quelqu'un casser la fenêtre
h les filles jouer au tennis.

Activity 2
1d, 2b, 3a, 4e, 5c.

Activity 3
1e, 2d, 3a, 4c, 5b.

Activity 4
a Après avoir pris une douche, elle a mis . . .
b Après avoir trouvé un parking, Charles et Patricia ont visité . . .
c Après s'être reposé, mon grand-père a fait . . .
d Après avoir fait ses courses, Madame Lebrun est allée . . .
e J'ai mis ma montre avant de me lever.
f Manon a caché le cadeau avant de sortir . . .
g Nous nous sommes baignés avant de manger . . .
h Ils sont allés à la poste avant de se promener . . .

Activity 5
a en attendant
b En regardant la photo
c tout en parlant à mon oncle
d en cherchant dans le garage
e En traversant la rue
f en lavant des voitures.

▼ *Verbs*

Activity 1
Ma mère et moi, nous sommes ici . . .
Je ne suis pas . . .
Antoine est plus grand . . .
Grégoire et toi, vous êtes dans . . .
Tu es fatigué?
Les deux magasins sont fermés . . .

Activity 2
a viennent
b arrive
c travaille
d vont
e va
f veulent.

Activity 3
demandes, aimons, adore, nage, jouent, promènent, restez, descendez, invite, écoutons, vends, pense, joues, finit, retrouvons, allons, choisissons, laisse, attendons, embrasse.

Activity 4
arriverez, donnerons, commencerez, garderons, décidera, devrez, aiderez, descendra, répondrez, demanderons, aurons, arriveront, montrerai, faudra, ferez, attendrons, arrivera.

Activity 5
ferais, appellerais, téléphonerais, appellerait, téléphonerait, feriez, volerait, ferions, pourrait, irions, enverraient, viendrait, laisserait, arriverait, laisserait, viendrait, faudrait.

Activity 6
étais, avaient, habitions, avait, se levait, réveillait, devais, buvais, mangeais, donnait, allait, aidais, faisions, vendions, venaient, écoutaient, allais, aimais, parlais, faisait, donnais.

Activity 7
frappa = *knocked*, attendit = *waited*, répondit = *answered*, appela = *called*, aboyèrent = *barked*, demanda = *asked*, courut = *ran*, traversèrent = *walked through*, s'installèrent = *settled down*, se coucha = *lay down*, apportèrent = *brought*, mangèrent = *ate*.

Activity 8
suis arrivé, est venu, avons pris, suis sorti, ai vu, ai acheté, est rentré, avons parlé, a préparé, avons mangé, me suis promené, a acheté, avez donné, as lavé, s'est réveillé.

Activity 9
s'est réveillé, a regardé, était couvert, brillait, avait, s'est habillé, a mis, est sorti, venaient, attendaient, a jeté, a mis, buvait, s'est approché, a eu, est parti, a regardé, téléphonait, est rentré.

Activity 10

a	mises		f	perdus
b	invités		g	lus
c	achetés		h	trouvé (no PDO)
d	vue		i	cassée
e	montré (no PDO)		j	choisis.

Activity 11

a	amusés		f	perdus
b	arrivée		g	restés
c	sortis		h	coupé
d	réveillée		i	tombée
e	embrassées		j	née

Activity 12
était arrivée, avait duré, étaient morts, avait dû, avions refusé, s'étaient séparés, avait ouvert, avait vu, avait pu.

Activity 13
Si nous avons le temps nous prendrons . . .
Si Eric . . . il aurait été malade.
Si vous gagniez . . . qu'est-ce que vous achèteriez?
S'il pleut tu peux . . .
Si elle m'expliquait . . . je pourrais . . .
Si tu t'étais cassé la jambe tu n'aurais pas pu . . .

Activity 14
je vienne (tu veux que)
je travaille (il faut que)
vous ne commenciez (avant que)
tu ne veuilles plus (à moins que)
ce soit (je préfère que)
je puisse (tu ne crois pas que)
qui sache (la seule . . .)
qui ait (le seul . . .)
tu dises (je n'aime pas que)
ce soit (qui que)
tu passes (Je préfère que)
on t'appelle (tu attends que)

Activity 15
a Prends!/Ne prends pas!
b réveille-toi!/ne te réveille pas!
c Attends!/N'attends pas!
d Ecoute!/N'écoute pas!
e Dépêche-toi!/Ne te dépêche pas!
f Répondez!/Ne répondez pas!
g Reposez-vous!/Ne vous reposez pas!
h Finissez!/Ne finissez pas!
i Mettez!/Ne mettez pas!
j Arrêtez-vous!/Ne vous arrêtez pas!

Activity 16
a Les prix seront distribués.
b La voiture avait été réparée.
c Les billets seront pris.
d Le voyage est payé.
e Le garage a été ouvert.
f L'argent serait perdu.
g La ville a été illuminée.
h Les valises auront été trouvées.

▼ Negatives, questions, exclamations

Activity 1
a Je ne vous connais pas.
b Il n'est pas reparti.
c Vous ne travaillez pas?
d Claude ne m'en a pas donné.
e Nous ne les reverrons pas demain.
f Elle n'attend pas Pascal.
g Vous n'y êtes pas allé?
h Mes parents ne me les ont pas achetés.

Activity 2
Elle n'est jamais sage . . . Je ne la voyais nulle part . . . Elle n'était plus . . . Elle n'était ni dans la cuisine ni dans la salle de bains . . . il n'y avait personne . . . il n'y avait que le chat . . . Je ne fais rien.

Activity 3
Vous passez/Est-ce que vous passez les vacances à Trouville?
Vous êtes française?/Est-ce que vous êtes française?
Vous avez loué/Est-ce que vous avez loué une maison?
Vous êtes venus/Est-ce que vous êtes venus en avion?
Vous êtes venue/Est-ce que vous êtes venue avec votre famille?
Vous avez/Est-ce que vous avez des frères?
Vous allez/Est-ce que vous allez tous les jours à la plage?
Vous avez vu/Est-ce que vous avez vu la fête du 14 juillet?
Vous voulez revenir/Est-ce que vous voulez revenir l'année prochaine?

Activity 4
Qu'est-ce qui, Qu'est-ce que, Qui, qu'est-ce que, qu'est-ce qu' . . . , Quelle,
laquelle, qu'est-ce que, Quelle, laquelle.

Activity 5
A quelle heure est-ce que, où, A quelle heure est-ce qu' . . . , comment,
Pourquoi est-ce qu' . . . , Pourquoi est-ce que, A quelle heure est-ce qu' . . .

Activity 6
a   . . . a-t-il demandé.
b   . . . répond-elle.
c   . . . ont crié les enfants.
d   . . . a déclaré Madame Jouvence.
e   . . . disais-je.
f   . . . a-t-elle demandé.
g   . . . a-t-il répondu.
h   . . . a annoncé Robert.

▼▼▼ INDEX